Magical

How Magic and its Star Performers Transformed the Entertainment Economy

by

Bharat Rao

Thank you for your purchase of this book!

As a token of my appreciation, I am pleased to provide you a FREE DOWNLOAD titled:

**10 BEST LIVE MAGIC SHOWS
to see in the USA 2019-2010**

Please visit the URL below to download your free copy.

https://magicalthebook.com/magicshows

A Note from the Author:

If you enjoy this book, please leave your honest review on Amazon, and do consider purchasing the ebook and audiobook versions.

As an author, I would like to hear from you, and your review provides me valuable information, feedback and encouragement. Your reviews and recommendations also help others like you to discover this book and related titles. You can sign up for news and updates through the book blog link below. Read on!

Links:

Book Website: https://magicalthebook.com/

Book Blog: https://magicalthebook.com/book-blog/

Amazon Author Page: http://amazon.com/author/bharatrao

The moment you doubt whether you can fly, you cease for ever to be able to do it.

—J.M. Barrie, Peter Pan

Table of Contents

Acknowledgements. ix

Preface. xiii

Chapter 1: The Global Renaissance of Magic. 1

Introduction 1

The State of the Magic Market and the $20,000 gig 5

Beetle Charms and Psychonauts:
Magic through the ages. 15

Becoming A Modern Magician 26

Chapter 2: They Made it Happen. 31

Magic in the Popular Culture in the US. 31

Robert-Houdin to David Blaine:
The Pioneers of Modern Magic. 37

Misdirection, Sleight of Hand,
and the link to Neuroscience 54

Chapter 3: The Penn and Teller Effect:
Modest Beginnings to the Pinnacle of Success 67

The Penn and Teller Effect 67

The Early Days 77

Expanding the Audience:
Going Public and Forays in Television 81

Becoming a Recognized National Brand 86

Chapter 4: The *BS* Years to *Fool Us* 91

BS: The Show Concept. 91

The Debunkers and the Debunked 94

The Fool Us Phenomenon: The Show Concept 99

Seasons 1 and 2:
Jonathan Ross and the British Invasion 101

Retaining the Creative Edge 105

Season 3-5:
Alyson Hannigan and the Move to Las Vegas 106

Chapter 5: Key Success Lessons 109

Creativity and seeking new challenges. 109

Persistence pays, especially if you are obsessive 114

Ability to look beyond the immediate 117

Mastering Control and Improvisation 119

Willingness to open up the platform
and recognize others 121

Promoting magic and inspiring young people 123

Ability to scale without sacrificing original identity
and style 124

Perfecting the Business Model 125

Chapter 6: Conclusions 129

A Business and Cultural Phenomenon 129

Expanding the size of the market. 133

Implications for other businesses. 135

What Does the Future Hold? 142

Afterword 151

References 155

About the Author 167

Appendix 1: A Magic Bill 169

Appendix 2: A Magic Proclamation 173

Acknowledgements

Several people were extremely generous with their time and resources during the writing of this book. For their insights into the roles of magicians and stage performers, I would like to thank Ryan Hayashi and Joshua Jay. You may know Ryan from his performance of the Ultimate Coin Matrix on *Penn and Teller: Fool Us*. Though a Canadian based in Germany, he certainly fooled me with his grasp of the cultural nuances of the American magic industry, as well as his fluency in a dozen languages. Joshua was extremely kind with his time and had well thought out answers to my questions, as well as honest feedback and encouragement. Other magicians I talked to were willing to discuss their hopes and expectations, as well as their fears and concerns in this new era of magic – you know who you are. For his insights into the Las Vegas entertainment industry, I thank Prof. David Schwartz, Director of the Gaming Lab at the University of Nevada, Las Vegas. For his help during the research and writing of this manuscript, I would like to thank Navil Zaman. Laura Vanderkam provided me valuable insights into the publishing process for which I am grateful. I should note that I would have been unable to write this book without the vast bibliographic resources of the Bobst Library at New York University, and the unending stream of archival footage available on YouTube.

New York, NY

January 6th, 2019

For Mira, Kieran &
Ruth

Preface

Penn and Teller have been performing for over four decades, and have reached the pinnacle of success through their live performances, TV appearances, and more recently, their popular TV show, Fool Us. While I had been familiar with their act since my days in graduate school in the nineties, and did sporadically watch their TV series, Penn and Teller BS, I did not follow them much until recently. It was only thanks to my kids that I discovered their newest incarnation. Watching a few tricks on a Fool Us episode before bedtime was for a while a favorite ritual for my kids, and as a result, alongside them, I had the pleasure of being entertained by the steady stream of conjurers who attempt to fool their genial and occasionally inscrutable hosts. As a fan of magic performances from a young age, I have long been curious about its history, it's incredible range of quirky characters and their skills, and its ability to create astonishment among fans of all ages. As an academic, my research primarily deals with emerging technologies and how they impact society. We have access to technologies and tools today that seem completely magical indeed. You can summon dinner or a ride or a gift for your friend through a swipe of your finger, look up the qualifications of your dentist, or book an impromptu vacation all without missing a beat. Many of the gadgets and interfaces we use would not only be unrecognizable to our predecessors from a few decades ago, they would surprise and indeed shock them with their 'magical' powers. Yet, even in the midst of such wonders of technology, we look forward to the performance of magic for its own sake, and constantly yearn for the sense of astonishment and wonder that it can create. In this book, I explore the impact of magic and magical thinking, and examine the impact of the magic industry in pushing the boundaries of what is possible, in some cases with sophisticated technology and gadgetry, but mostly employing simple methods of manipulating our attention, perception, and use of cognitive resources. I also discuss how the techniques and skills developed by top magicians can be translated to the world of business innovation, as firms seek to come up with unique solutions to customer problems, at the intersection of design, technology, and service.

Today, magic is becoming a major part of the entertainment economy, as evidenced by the increased share of revenues, widespread interest in popular media, and the improved career prospects for dedicated and talented performers. David Copperfield, Penn and Teller, David Blaine and others are among the superstars in this industry, and are seasoned entrepreneurs running global entertainment businesses. Through their success, they have become role models to many of their peers, even as they remain fiercely competitive. I wanted to investigate the secrets of their success, as well as outline the path they have paved for other magicians and performers hoping to gain an entry into this lucrative industry. Having spent time in the past as a case writer at Harvard Business School, and as an academic researcher at NYU, I immediately began to sketch out all the interesting angles one could look at, and soon found that there are many layers to this story and it is one worth telling. This book documents the transformational change in the sphere of professional magic in recent decades, its broader connection to popular entertainment and media, and the changing perceptions of and expectations from magic performers in the minds of the public. The idea behind this book was to use the Penn and Teller phenomenon, and particularly their TV show, Fool Us, as a lens through which we could examine the wider magic industry, and its impact on the popular imagination. The "success secrets" followed by leading magicians like David Copperfield, Penn and Teller, and David Blaine, among others, both as professional magicians, recognizable brands and formidable business owners can be applied by entrepreneurs, business people and self-starters who want to make a mark in their careers. I also explore the allure of magic in our modern times, both as a form of entertainment and recreation, and also for its ability to inspire us to be creative and think outside the box.

Mostly, I wrote this book to satisfy my own curiosity, and to find out more about a topic I have always been interested in, both as an amateur dabbler in magic, and as a fan of a polished magic performance. I also wanted to make more explicit the connections between the practice of magic as a performance art, to the skills required to run a successful startup or new product development project. Many of the performances described in this book can be viewed on YouTube, which also contains vast resources for the aspiring magician. To conduct more in-depth research on this book, I was able to access voluminous archives from the vast literature on magic, interview magicians with very different approaches to their performance, and access accounts of the magic business from the trade and business media. While these may yet not present the entire picture, we can start discovering what lies under the hood, or perhaps more aptly, 'behind the curtain' of this diverse and dynamic industry. In the process, I have found that the field of magic, which already has a rich and complex history going back centuries, is currently enjoying a renaissance of sorts with the help of star performers, TV platforms and forums for them to show off their craft, the rise of social media, and easy access to content and knowledge made possible by the Information Age. Magic has always been mixed in with generous helpings from the dark and supernatural sides, despite the general thrust of modern magic to be on the secular dimension. We find that magic is also a fertile ground for a wide array of ambitious and eccentric personalities, many of whom dedicate their entire lives to advancing obscure areas of magical endeavor that most of us would not even realize ever existed, and would not know what to do with it if we did. What unites them however is their unending quest to discover, improve and invent new ways of causing delight, mystification, wonder and entertainment for their audience.

We are indeed living in a golden age of magical arts and performance. I hope you enjoy reading this book as much as I have enjoyed writing it.

Chapter 1:
The Global Renaissance of Magic

Reality seems so simple. We just open our eyes and there it is. But that doesn't mean it is simple.

—Teller

If you want to talk about magic, the stuff that blows me away is the stuff that's done close up.

—Penn Jillette

Introduction

Every magician aspires to pull off a trick that will be memorable, and will truly mystify and entertain their audience. In order to do this, they need to carefully master the critical elements that are needed for each 'trick', study the work of previous magicians who have performed the same or similar routines, and put in hours of patient practice and fine tuning. This requires a range of skills, the foremost of them being creativity, discipline, persistence and self-confidence. Once they have mastered the underlying technique, the next challenge is to put together a convincing performance that shows off their hard-won ability to create a convincing effect for the audience. Perhaps the best description of the premise and the process of putting together a successful act comes from

Christopher Priest, who wrote the book The Prestige, which was later turned into a blockbuster film directed by Christopher Nolan. As Priest puts it:

"Every great magic trick consists of three parts or acts. The first part is called "The Pledge". The magician shows you something ordinary: a deck of cards, a bird or a man. He shows you this object. Perhaps he asks you to inspect it to see if it is indeed real, unaltered, normal. But, of course... it probably isn't.

The second act is called "The Turn". The magician takes the ordinary something and makes it do something extraordinary. Now you're looking for the secret... but you won't find it, because of course you're not really looking. You don't really want to know. You want to be fooled. But you wouldn't clap yet. Because making something disappear isn't enough; you have to bring it back.

That's why every magic trick has a third act, the hardest part, the part we call "The Prestige."

—Christopher Priest, The Prestige

Two common misconceptions of magic are that magicians seek to trick or deceive the audience, and possibly promote the supernatural. Although we use the term 'trick' liberally when talking about magic, in reality, what magicians are focused on is in creating the illusion of impossibility. Most magicians today dislike claiming that their work deals with the supernatural as it will only end up damaging their aesthetic and identity as creators of the impossible. They also want to be the first to dissociate themselves with the darker connotations of magic. However, in many cases, these performers do rely on visual, optical, and cognitive illusions, special effects (like gunshots, explosions, etc.), and secret devices or gimmicks to execute their tricks. Visual illusions rely on the brain's misperception of what is seen, optical illusions rely on tricks of light with no tricking of the brain per se, and cognitive illusions rely on manipulation of higher level brain functions (most coin and card tricks are cognitive illusions). By using these techniques, they give us the impression that they are doing impossible things, and we in the audience are sophisticated enough to know it as we enjoy the effects. However, this phenomenon is only true with modern magic. Most historical accounts of magic do not draw such a clear distinction between the real and the supernatural, and as we shall see, magic has been used as a vehicle for perpetuating a variety of dubious and unverifiable claims over its centuries of existence. The word magic itself has therefore carried negative connotations throughout much of history. By contrast, the modern or secular magic that we encounter today must thus be seen as a performance at best, but a sophisticated one at that. As Teller, of the magic duo, Penn and Teller, explains, "Magic is a form of theater that depicts impossible events as though they were really happening." Magic, unlike traditional entertainment, suggests that an event is really happening, while traditional entertainment alludes to stories that could happen. Therefore, an audience must believe an act to be impossible in order for the magician to contradict their understanding of reality. To expand on Teller's statement, magic does not just depict the impossible, it appears to present it as simultaneously real and unreal. Thus, it creates an interesting conundrum for the viewer. We will still call this a trick, mostly as a matter of convenience. Magic pulls viewers in two opposing directions: it coerces the audience to try and explain an event, but the performance itself tries to prevent them from finding an explanation. According to magician Whit Haydn, magic traps viewers in a logical conundrum, and viewers keep coming back to the illusion because they cannot understand it (and want to make sense of it). In parallel, magicians employ carefully synchronized talk or patter, which essentially involves manipulation of the audience's attention and expectations, further confusing them. Also, because our ability to form an explanation depends on what we know, the skilled magician relies on the systematic blocking of explanations based on their knowledge of who is in the audience, and an understanding of how they would explain it with what they know. Thus, experienced magicians are shrewd in that they always suggest a number of possible explanations for a trick, none of them completely conclusive. As Eric Mead, a gifted close-up magician who appeared twice on *Penn and Teller: Fool Us* explained it during one of his performances, if there is sufficient ambiguity about 10% of the trick (i.e. 90% of the trick can be explained clearly), that is enough for even a fellow conjurer to be fooled by the trick. Creating this doubt is always better than presenting something so astounding that the audience clearly senses a clever contraption or tricked up effect. By focusing on the weakest link in the chain, even the most experienced magician can thus be fooled. The essayist and performer Jamy Ian Swiss has distilled the essence of good magic tricks to five key ingredients. These include: audience involvement, the creation of an emotional hook, the visuality of the effect, inherent humor in its delivery, and high concept. In his book, *Shattering Illusions*, he describes in detail how the mastery of each of these elements can play a vital role in pulling off a memorable routine.

Consider any performance by a magician in a typical Penn and Teller *Fool Us* episode, which you can watch online or on TV, and if you are fortunate enough, from a cozy seat at the Rio Hotel and Casino in Las Vegas. You follow along and understand the pledge, the magician next demonstrates the turn, which you may or may not completely follow, but you and the rest of the audience know that the final twist is coming. The prestige can make or break the trick, but this is the climax that everyone has been waiting for. We expect and perhaps wish for the magician to fool Penn and Teller, but on the other hand you also expect to discover the secret of the trick before they do. A lot of it has to do with the psychology of magic performance itself. The human mind generally believes what the eyes see, but if what you are seeing is unbelievable, your brain is immediately sent into overdrive trying to decipher how it was done. Being experienced magic hands, Penn and Teller have literally seen thousands of tricks during their careers, and performed a vast majority of them as well. As ardent practitioners, they are well aware of the hacks that magicians use to trick the eye and the brain. Despite all that, the format of the show encourages magicians to come up with their best, knowing full well that they may not be able to fool their hosts. It also forces them to innovate on known routines, or create completely new ones. It is indeed an entertaining battle of wits on stage, and as judges, Penn and Teller cannot afford to blink or they will surely be led down blind alleys cleverly designed by the magician who is out to fool them.

In this book, we will examine how the magic industry has changed over the years, the strides made by its major performers, and in parallel, the perception of magicians themselves in the popular culture. We then look at the contributions of major performers in the history of magic, and how there is a definite progression in the field's evolution. Following this, we will consider the specific case of Penn and Teller, who currently represent the faces of magic in the popular culture. We will explore the evolution of the Penn and Teller brand, and describe how they have surmounted various obstacles to achieve fame and fortune. In their latest reincarnation, they appear in a show well into its fifth season *Penn and Teller– Fool Us*. The show has garnered widespread acclaim and turned them into not just national icons but global brands. Over the past forty years, Penn and Teller have established a stellar reputation as successful stage performers and larger-than-life personalities, and they command the devotion and loyalty of a legion of fans. Today, they serve as the gatekeepers and curators of a continuous parade of old and new magicians as they try and make a mark on a global stage and platform. Through their performances and TV shows, they continue to serve as leading advocates and educators of magic, and have been instrumental in the discovery of new talent. We also explore what I call the Penn and Teller effect, i.e. the effect that a successful performance on *Fool Us* creates for a diverse range of magicians. Shows like Fool Us, and versions of the *Got Talent* franchise, particularly *America's Got Talent* and *Britain's Got Talent* have put magic back on the entertainment map, by offering a global platform for talented performers. In 2019, CBS is slated to debut a new talent, *The World's Best*, which will feature performers from several genres, who will be judged by experts in over fifty categories. We then look at the underlying factors that help magicians learn over time and craft their performance, eventually leading to long term success. We conclude by looking at how these success factors can be applied to any business setting, both in small startups as well as in larger firms.

The State of the Magic Market and the $20,000 gig

Las Vegas has a long tradition of residencies by leading artists, particularly musicians, and now a growing group of high-profile magicians. One of the earliest musical stars who catapulted to fame using this method was Liberace, who was making fifty thousand dollars a week in 1955. Dubbed "Mr. Showmanship", Liberace would thrill audiences with his impressively staged entrances and exits, expert piano playing, all while flashing his extra-large diamond studded rings and commenting to the audience, "I hope you like 'em; you bought 'em!". Elvis Presley soon followed, and in one inspired streak, played 636 consecutive (and sold-out) performances at the International and the Hilton. The first ensemble effort to achieve major success was The Rat Pack, who held sway over the Sands' Copa Room. Although this was an informal group which played for a short amount of time, members of the group became popular cultural icons. The star-studded entertainers in this group included Frank Sinatra, Dean Martin, Sammy Davis Jr., Joey Bishop and Peter Lawford, each of whom could command record audiences on their own. Lawford was also President John F. Kennedy's brother-in-law, and the President himself was a frequent visitor. Their impromptu events in Las Vegas would attract high rollers to the casinos at short notice, and they had an immediate impact on multiple streams of tourist revenues starting with gambling. The Rat Pack also starred in several Hollywood movies including Ocean's 11, Sergeants 3, and Robin and the 7 Hoods. Collectively, with the Count Basie Orchestra playing in the background, they took Vegas by storm, and are considered till today to be the original drivers of the entertainment brand of Las Vegas itself. Fast forwarding to more contemporary times, the most successful performer in Vegas, Wayne Newton, has played thousands of times over his career, while Celine Dion, who started her residency in 2003, had played more than seven hundred shows by 2007 and sold $400 million worth of tickets. Others well-known names like Elton John (take home of $500,000 per show) and Mariah Carey ($330,000 per show) make up the ever-increasing cast of musical talent that calls Vegas home. Siegfried and Roy arrived on the Las Vegas scene in 1967, debuting at the Stardust in "Lido De Paris". They went on to create and star in one of the most popular and successful shows, and were also the first put magic firmly on the entertainment map. A number of the top performers in magic today can thank Las Vegas for their fame and fortunes.

Residencies are attractive for the casinos, which have now morphed into all-purpose resorts where gambling is just one of the many activities on offer. The resorts do not need to spend additional money on promotion as many of these performers are established brands with a strong fan base. They serve as anchor tenants in flagship properties and drive room occupancy, as well as spending on merchandising, retail and restaurants, thus optimizing the use of every square foot of space within the property. For the performers, a longer-term residency gives them the ability to set down roots, raise families, and not have to deal with the hassle of constant travel. The proximity to Los Angeles and Hollywood are a further incentive to the big-name performers who also work in film or TV.

The magic market today is constituted by a range of performers, from the superstars who rake in millions every year, to individual acts who may perform part-time, and for whom magic may not be a primary source of income. Several household names dominate the list of headliners. Until recently, it was hard to obtain detailed information on earnings and the scale of individual operations. First in 2017, and then again in 2018, Forbes Magazine published a list of the world's top magicians based on a more in-depth analysis. The key findings from these reports are presented below. I then discuss how the market gets further fragmented as we move down the line, as well as the typical sources of income for magicians. All the data presented in this section is from public domain sources including surveys, newspaper reports and websites. While the size of the magic audience is by no means comparable to that of music, we can still get an instructive look at the state of big name magic by considering its top performers and their typical activities and revenues. Not surprisingly, many of them are based in Las Vegas for a good part of the year. Las Vegas has thus played an instrumental role in creating a market for big-name magic, and also a continued role for magic in the entertainment economy, both locally and worldwide.

By the end of 2018, Las Vegas was expected to host over forty-two million visitors, of which around 6.6 million were convention attendees, as per data from the Las Vegas Convention and Visitors Authority. Of these, nearly 16% of the visitors were international, 21% were first time visitors, and almost 38% were millennials. Over the past two decades, as the profile of visitors underwent significant changes, the gambling revenues in Vegas, which used to account for nearly 60 percent of tourist revenues has fallen to around 35%.

By the end of summer 2018, major casino operators reported declines in revenues per available room, an industry metric used to assess the profitability of Vegas casinos. In parallel, related metrics like room occupancy as well as convention attendance were also down. Convention attendees for example, are less likely to gamble as much as other visitors, and also contribute more to revenues from dining and entertainment. A number of factors have driven this change. As David Schwartz, Director of the Gaming Lab at the University of Nevada at Las Vegas, explained to me, Las Vegas and Reno were the traditionally considered the prime destinations for gamblers, but that is no longer the case. A proliferation of gaming options around the United States means that people don't have to go to Vegas to gamble. In fact, nearly twenty percent of visitors to Vegas don't gamble at all. Schwartz points out that the design of the casinos themselves have changed in response to the changing demand factors. Previously they looked like big air-conditioned boxes focused purely on gaming. Now the design has been flipped inside out, with a number of options adjacent to the gambling. These include luxury shopping, fine restaurants, and other retail activity. Prime examples include the Link (Caesars Entertainment), and the area around the New York, New York 2 area (MGM Grand Resorts). Further, the changing financial structure of building casinos, where the cost has ballooned to the billions of dollars from a few hundreds of millions. This means that there is a greater premium being placed on non-gambling revenue options right from the planning phases of these projects.

What has changed despite the continuing declines in gambling revenues in Las Vegas is that the entertainment sector has taken up the slack, resulting in blockbuster shows by leading names, and the increased willingness of promoters and impresarios to invest in new talent. Big name magic shows have been direct beneficiaries of these trends. As far as the casinos and resorts are concerned, there is a lot more competition for wallet share of the consumer with an intense focus on understanding where they shop, where they eat, and what kind of shows and entertainment they may patronize. Serious fans may plan an entire trip to Las Vegas based on a single show they plan to see (e.g. Celine Dion, David Copperfield, or Penn and Teller, for instance). However, data from the Las Vegas Convention Authority shows that the vast majority of tourists usually decide where they will eat or on entertainment options only when they are in Vegas, and frequently on the day of the show itself. As Vegas continues to attract more diverse audiences, there is an immense appetite for an equally varied menu of entertainment options. Alongside live music, magic has become one of the mainstays and prime beneficiaries of these trends, and the steady commercial rise of many of the leading practitioners needs to be seen with this in mind. In this section, we look mainly at the top US based magicians, and those on whom earnings data is available readily, especially for 2017 and 2018. In a future section, I also discuss the state of magic in another major market, the UK. This will be in the context of Penn and Teller's Season 1 of the show *Fool Us*, which was focused mainly on magicians practicing there.

In 2018, the top seven highest-paid magic acts brought in combined annual revenues $149 million, before taxes and fees. David Copperfield was the world's highest paid magician, and made $61 million pretax for the twelve months ended June 2018, a slight decline from the $61.5 million pretax in 2017. This was the second consecutive year he held the title. His sources of income in the year included 670 shows performed at the MGM Grand in Las Vegas, private tours and concerts, revenues from his private island resort, Masha Cay in the Bahamas, which has been called the most luxurious resort in the world, and his Museum of Magic. Including Musha Cay, Copperfield is the owner of a total of 11 islands in the Bahamas as part of his real estate holdings. They have been rebranded as the "Islands of Copperfield Bay", and the resort charges its celebrity guests up to $37,500 a night. Visitors to his properties there include names like Bill Gates, Oprah Winfrey, John Travolta and Sergey Bring. The richest magician in history, his net worth in 2018 was estimated to be $875 million. Penn and Teller came in second in 2018 at $30 million, also a slight decline from their 2017 earnings of $30.5 million pretax. In 2017, they performed 254 shows in Las Vegas at over $100,000 worth of income a night, and have been residents at the Rio Hotel and Casino, where they have had the longest-running show in Vegas history. That year, they also finished their fourth season of *Penn and Teller: Fool Us*. Criss Angel came in third with $16 million in income, which was higher than the $14.5 million earned in 2017. During the year prior, he had been touring with his "Mindfreak Live" with Cirque du Soleil, performing 10 shows a week at the Luxor Hotel (Las Vegas), doing a handful of private shows, and working on his new TV show Criss Angel: Trick'd Up. His income was a bit lower than prior year because his tour prevented him from booking more events. He also owns a traveling revue, The Supernaturalists, which did not go on tour that year, thus detracting from his earnings. His Luxor contract was for 10 years, and ended in 2017.

In 2018, David Blaine came in fourth, more than doubling his earnings to $13.5 million, compared to $6 million in 2018. The highlight of the year was a sold-out North American tour which brought in close to $12 million. Despite performing only 50 shows, a good part of the revenue was driven by merchandise sales and VIP packages that included meet-and-greets with guests. Blaine used to make most of his money from private corporate shows, but the success of his recent tour shows that he has grown a strong core following among fans. Next in line at No. 5 were the Illusionists, comprising a set of rotating magicians, performed over 350 shows globally and brought in $12 million. One of the highlights of the year was Shin Lim's winning the America's Got Talent competition. Lim is one of the star magicians of the group. In the prior year, they held the fourth position with earnings of $11.5 million. Their Broadway show was the most successful magic show in history raking in $2.4 million in the first week. At sixth and seventh place were Michael Carbonaro and Derren Brown with earnings of $8.5 million and $8 million. Each had a TV show and popular tours, and Carbonaro had published multiple books and made an off-Broadway theatrical debut. Brown also stars in a new Netflix special, Sacrifice.

In 2017, Dynamo had come in fifth with $9 million in earnings, a number that has decreased by half after his "Seeing is Believing" tour had ended in the prior year. But he did arena shows in Australia as well as private shows, and developed a brand partnership with FC Barcelona. However, in 2018, he dropped off the list of the top performers due to his ongoing battle with Crohn's disease. I discuss more about popular British magicians in a future section.

Performer	Earnings
David Copperfield	$61m
Penn and Teller	$30m
Criss Angel	$16m
David Blaine	$13.5m
The Illusionists	$12m
Michael Carbonaro	$8.5m
Darren Brown	$8m

Table 1: Top 7 magicians in order of earnings (ending June 2018)

As we can see, most of the big-name magicians have carved out their own special niche, but also rely on multiple sources of income. Typically, there is a split between live performances in fixed locations (like Las Vegas), performances for private groups and at events, and revenues from activities like TV shows and merchandising, and educational videos and courses in some cases. At the fixed location shows, there can be further segmentation of the offerings, based on customer profiles, and the ability of the performers to offer tiered packages that offer unique engagement or pre- and post-show options. We will discuss this further in a future section. There are also a number of magicians whose primary revenue source is creating new tricks for sale, both to professional magicians and to the public, and several do have an active performance oriented business. They can remain behind the scenes, so to speak, while still operating at the top of their game, but catering mainly to the business-to-business end of the market (i.e. delivering tricks and props to other magicians). They are still actively engaged in research and development (of creating new tricks, routines and shows), promotion and public relations (through their media appearances), and the eventual production and sale of their end products (new shows, TV specials or manufacturing and selling props, for example). From time to time, some of them also develop tricks for sale for the mass market, and market it through social media, including popular venues like YouTube and Instagram.

Finding a niche where one can excel, both in terms of audience fit, and earnings potential, seems to be extremely important for those seeking careers as full-time magicians, whether as stage or close-up performers. This is how many magicians start, and frequently remain for their entire careers. Others can get a lucky break that helps them put their careers on a different gear, and leads to improved or extended streams of revenue. One great example of this is Steve Cohen, the self-styled "Millionaire's Magician". In 2003, Cohen was a broke professional magician, earning around $1,500 per show. Then he met Mark Levy, a positioning consultant, who told him "If you take the $2,000 gig, you won't get the $20,000 gig." Levy later became Cohen's creative director, and together they developed the "Millionaire's Magician" persona. Levy and Cohen discovered that there was a lucrative gap in the market—there were very few acts which catered to small but very wealthy groups of individuals (i.e. the super-rich). Once Cohen appeared on CBS Sunday Morning touting this concept, his popularity dramatically increased, netting him $1 million in ticket sales by the end of the week. Cohen has performed for more than half a million guests over his career, including big-name clients like Michael Bloomberg, Prince Sultan bin Saud of Saudi Arabia, Warren Buffett, Stephen Sondheim, Guillermo del Toro, and the Queen of Morocco. He performs at the Lotte New York Palace Hotel, delivering a high-end private show "Chamber Magic" for wealthy, well-dressed attendees. The shows are usually sold out, and Cohen continues to expand his unique portfolio of tricks, frequently testing and adding new routines. He says that he enjoys performing, and never expected to be this successful. In honor of his five thousandth performance, New York City mayor Bill de Blasio designated October 6th as "Chamber Magic Day" as a special honor for this achievement. Cohen went on to star in a History Channel documentary about the origins of magic. As Cohen has discovered, once he gained entry into an exclusive network of clients, word-of-mouth and network effects then took over, and his business snowballed. He has also put his creative energies to work in creating a graphic novel, titled The Millionaires' Magician, which features him in a fictionalized role as a crime fighter and superhero.

Despite the impressive revenues generated by the top players, not all magic performers are household names, make seven figure incomes, or have jet setting lifestyles to boot. Most magicians are still small scale performers who do walk-around or parlor magic. Most of the money they make come from performances at schools, private parties, and corporate events. Out of the 15,000 members of the International Brotherhood of Magicians, 20% were professional magicians. Good professional magicians in big cities can make over $100,000 annually by doing corporate events. Shawn Farquhar, ex-president of the International Brotherhood of Magicians, makes $250,000 from private shows in America and Asia (he has fooled Penn and Teller twice on his *Fool Us* appearances). Many successful professional magicians thus make between six and seven figures annually. Aaron Radatz makes seven figures doing domestic and international shows while based in Las Vegas. When he was a teenager, he worked part-time doing small shows, and earned as much as a full-time fast food worker. He has a degree in marketing, and focuses on the business aspect of magic. His biggest sources of income are corporate events and casino and theme park shows. He says that most magicians are hobbyists, not businessmen, and if an area is saturated with magicians, the performer should move and try to find new opportunities. Focusing on and improving the quality of work leads to increased revenues. Designing custom props rather than purchasing commercial products can lead to lower expenses for the magician who is just starting out. For magicians who find the task of managing a business daunting, he also recommends working in a pair with a partner who understands the business aspects. This enables the primary member of the team to focus on the performance, or vice versa. Frank DeMasi is another full-time magician making six figures doing family shows and birthday parties. He, like Radatz, has branched into instructional magic. DeMasi makes a part of his income from sales of his "Magic Frank's Lessons in Magic." He says that with part time performers, you get what you pay for. The quality of the show scales with price and professional status. Most small-scale magicians purchase or license the illusions they use from designers and builders of magical effects, under the self-imposed magician's code of silence, which forbids them to reveal how the tricks work.

Greg Bordner, who owns Abbott's Magic Manufacturing Company (a popular prop manufacturer), says that the most important thing is to have a quality act, followed by a list of people to email and follow up on. In other words, they should have a platform and audience they can rely on, and who are invested in their brands. In addition, Bordner says that each successful magician must make a unique act that is to be kept secret at all costs. Because most career magicians have unique shows, *big name magicians are just small time magicians who have been discovered*. Max Darwin (Amazing Max) makes $200,000 annually, from anything ranging from corporate shows to birthday parties, and also does weekly off-Broadway shows on tour. He says that the more successful a magician is, the higher his rates go and the less he has to perform. With added flexibility, he is able to do more shows and family oriented magic, which he finds more gratifying than corporate events. Gary Ferrar, another NYC based magician, prefers smaller venues because of the intimacy of performing with more engaged crowds. Consequently, he has to work many more shows, with corporate events taking up the weekdays and weddings and birthday parties taking up the weekends. His rates vary from $1500 (corporate) to $500 (birthdays) per hour, and may increase depending on the audience. He has performed for celebrities like Michael Bloomberg and Robert De Niro, which he thinks has helped him with branding and networking and provided a boost to his popularity. Another performer who has benefited from the right connections is Jonathan Bayme, the founder of Theory11. Bayme has used his long experience in magic to create a show titled The Magician, that originally started with one live performance a week, but soon expanded to six per week. With high profile celebrity guests like Chelsea Clinton, Jesse Eisenberg, Jimmy Fallon and Kim Kardashian West, Bayme also serves as a successful performer as consultant to other magicians. As for the New York shows, tickets have frequently sold out within the first sixty seconds of release. In August of 2018, theory11 announced that they would debut a magic show in Los Angeles, starting Justin Willman. Willman, a well-known magician who appears frequently on TV, including on a Netflix original series titled *Magic For Humans*. In addition to such shows featuring celebrity appearances and aggressive promotion, there are a number of cities around the US where close-up magic has been a mainstay of nightlife entertainment. In New York, Monday Night Magic is the longest running off-Broadway show dedicated to magic. Every week, a rotating cast of magicians entertains a small crowd in an intimate setting at The Players Theater in Greenwich Village. Similarly, Chicago is the scene of a Magic Cabaret every Wednesday night at the Greenhouse Theater Center, and magic is the focus at other venues like the Magic Lounge and the Magic Parlor.

Performing for well-off clients usually provides a steady source of income, or increases popularity for other shows, as well as creates new lines or revenue through consulting and custom gigs. However, the majority of magicians are part time performers who perform as hobbyists or to earn supplemental income. One example, Liam Maleah, performs on weekends for fun, while working as a lawyer during the rest of the week. He is not concerned about generating money through his performances, as he performs purely for personal satisfaction. Hence the magic industry is extremely diversified, with a lot more fragmentation at the lower end of the value chain. In some cases, amateur and semi-professional magicians spend a number of years at that stage of the value chain and still derive great satisfaction from it. Others may take their magic another notch, and soon aim to hit the big leagues. One could argue that magic and magic performance is now a mature industry, with performers catering to every segment of the market, and also developing distinct niches and positioning within the field. The industry, like any other, is impacted by changes in culture, customer demand, and developments in technology, but very often has been at the forefront of driving change itself. In the following sections, we will see how magic has changed and evolved over the ages, and how the modern magic industry as we know it has come to be, mainly through to impressive contributions by several landmark performers, many of whom are household names today.

Beetle Charms and Psychonauts: Magic through the ages

Magical thinking has been with us since ancient times, and has been practiced across cultures. Art historians and anthropologists theorize that Paleolithic cave paintings that depict human and animal forms were not just a form of magical thinking, but also represented their deep held cultural beliefs, including the embodiments of ancestral spirits. Perhaps one of the best examples of this from ancient civilizations where we have clear records is the ancient Egyptian Book of the Dead (1500 BCE to 50 BCE), where the paintings and hieroglyphs depict images of magical spells, which the ancient Egyptians believed would facilitate the crossing of the soul into the underworld. These spells were also used in daily life to "bind" people to various outcomes, and weren't just verbal in nature. Believers paid magicians to give them talismans that they could use to convert their desires and intentions into physical manifestation. They were frequently carried around on one's person, thus making amulets a much sought after fashion accessory. Nearly five thousand years old, the Westcar Papyrus, which is on display at the Egyptian Museum in Berlin, records the story of magical feats performed by priests and magicians and is referred to as "King Cheops and the Magicians". In it, the magician Djedi performs feats like reattaching severed animal heads and taming wild lions, besides making startling prophecies about the future dynasty. Djedi's ability to reanimate animals by re-attaching their severed heads was one of the most puzzling mysteries in magic until it was rediscovered and performed in the 1800s. Today, a modern version of the trick is performed by the gifted English magician, Ali Cook, in his 'Hen and Ducks' routine. Similarly, the use of spells and talismans continue to the present day despite their questionable efficacy. As Stuart Vyse, a psychologist and author of "Believing in Magic: The Psychology of Superstition" observes, in times of dire need, people do turn to irrational beliefs, and frequently they turn to superstitions, magic, religion and the paranormal. Similarly, Dr. Ted Kaptchuk, who oversees Harvard University's program in placebo studies and the therapeutic encounter, believes that the power of suggestion can be a strong motivator. He has personally participated in multiple studies that show that placebos, rituals, and talismans play a modest role in helping patients feel better, compared to surgery and medication. This does not mean that there is any established scientific cause and effect, but simply that hope and belief can drive seemingly irrational behavior. In our modern societies where celebrities and celebrity culture are celebrated (instead of gods and goddesses), sociologists see parallels to more primitive practices. By getting close to celebrities or buying relics associated with the stars, the fan hopes to acquire the celebrity's power through a process of transference, just like the ancients did with their amulets and talismans.

Moving on from ancient Egypt and looking further down the timeline of the ancient world, there are plenty of references to magic in ancient Semitic, Old Persian, Aramaic, and Chaldean languages, each with slightly different connotations. The Greek philosopher Herodotus describes how the Persian *mágoi*, who were royal advisors, and were in charge of performing religious rites and aided in dream interpretation. Through these ancient languages, we see magic arriving into Greek and Latin and continuing its evolution. Magic in Europe has had a long history, and has been a part of many cultures from ancient times to the present. For example, the magical tradition in England similarly stretches nearly five thousand years, from the shamen of the Neolithic era, the Anglo-Saxon wyrd-crafters, to more modern Wiccans and New Age spiritualists. Recently, several scholars have been reconstructing the history of witchcraft and magic in Ireland despite the dearth of original source material. In Iceland, another country with a centuries-old tradition in the practice of witchcraft and sorcery, magic spells were used for various purposes, domestic and communal. During the Viking age, the magic rituals included both female and male practitioners, called "vísendakona" (the woman of science), and "seið-menn" (the men of magic ritual). Together, they participated in shamanic ceremonies that involved alternate states of consciousness and journeys into other dimensions. These shamans were concerned with channeling power and knowledge from the gods during the rituals. An early distinction on the varieties of magic comes from Augustine of Hippo (A.D. 354-430), who separated miracles from magic, by considering the underlying agent causing the awe-inspiring effects. Miracles were attributed to God, and witnessing them was believed to cause greater adherence among the followers. Magic, on the other hand, was immoral and taboo, as it was attributed to demonic involvement.

Accounts of miracles and their records can be sketchy at best and are usually exaggerated through their retelling. A good example of this is the famous Indian rope-trick, where eyewitness accounts can be found from the fourteenth century and onward. In this trick, the magician throws up a rope into the air, whereupon it remains rigid. The magician's assistant (usually a small boy), climbs up this rigid rope, and disappears when he reaches the top. When he fails to materialize, the magician himself climbs up in search of the boy, but only dismembered body parts rain down followed by the magician. The parts are covered with a cloth, and the boy is revealed intact with a dramatic flourish. A study by Wiseman and Lamont found that historical eyewitness accounts of this trick tended to be exaggerated. In fact, the more the time that had passed between the witnessing of the trick and its recount, the greater was the degree of exaggeration. Hence, we have to take reports of miracles being witnessed with a grain of salt, and usually there is a more mundane explanation to account for the effects described, even by people who witnessed it in person. In his recent book, the Australia-based author and journalist John Zubrzycki points out the ancient origins of the magical arts in India. The Atharva Veda, a sacred Hindu text believed to have originated around 1400 BC, is said to have been composed by fire-priests skilled in performing magic rites. Even today, no serious religious ceremony in India can take place without a sacred fire-rite, with invocations that have been passed down over generations. Whether these are magical is a different question, but the belief is that done with the appropriate penance and dedication, special powers can indeed be called on to help. This is similar to the practice of 'white magic' that was practiced during the Renaissance, where the magician attempted to create an alliance with divine spirits, and ultimately with God. Thus, the fire-priest acts as an intermediary between the believer and the divine, and prescribes the correct materials and procedures to be followed during the rituals. Other sacred texts dating back to the eleventh century contain references to magic spells and the stories around them. The practice of magic in India has been deeply intertwined with religion and superstition and has been practiced by learned men as well as street-performers, thugs, tricksters and con men. By the late 1700s, Indian magicians were being shipped to London to entertain their British masters. As one British scribe put it, "The whole tribe of sleight-of-hand men in Europe are mere bunglers when compared with the jugglers in India". Soon these conscripted conjurers were delighting English audiences with effects from levitation and snake-charming to sword swallowing, while painting an exotic and somewhat distorted picture of the faraway colony. There has also been a long history of the practice of witchcraft and 'black magic' in India, with its exponents facing frequent persecutions. Interestingly, the practice of witchcraft and the violent reactions against it continue to this day. Over two thousand suspected witches were murdered between 2000 and 2012, as per records of the Indian National Crime Records Bureau. An average of 150 women per year are killed accused of being witches, especially in central India, a staggering number.

During the 15th and 16th century, there was a revival of interest in ceremonial magic. In 1456, Johannes Hartlieb, a royal Bavarian physician, outlined the seven *artes magicae* or *artes prohibitae*, which were acts explicitly prohibited by the canon law of the Church. These included necromancy, geomancy, hydromancy, aeromancy, pyromancy, chiromancy, and scapulimancy. These were different forms of divination based on the mediums used. While necromancy or demonic magic dealt with 'raising the dead', and performing divination with blood and corpses, the other categories were less controversial, dealing with divination using stones and sand (geomancy), water (hydromancy), air (aeromancy), fire (pyromancy), palm reading (chiromancy) and the scapula of animals (scapulimancy).

Magic has also played an integral part in the artistic and cultural landscape. One early painting by Hieronymus Bosch, titled 'The Conjurer,' which he created in 1502, shows a close-up magic performance featuring the age-old cups-and-balls routine. If you look closely, not only is the audience member at the front getting fooled by the magician, but one wonders if his pocket is also being picked by the audience member behind him, who is conveniently looking at the ceiling and practicing misdirection. Perhaps he is an aspiring conjurer himself!

The Conjurer, by Hieronymus Bosch, 1502

During the Renaissance, the famous painter Sandro Botticelli produced works that were considered to hold protective magical powers, and others that were meant to invoke the dark powers of magic. In his famous painting, La Primavera, which can be seen at the Uffizi museum in Florence, Botticelli depicts Venus, in a red robe, at the center of the frame. Although the exact meaning of the scene is still debated, some scholars believe that she depicts the benevolence that protects mankind. At the far left is Mercury, the Roman god of business merchants, travelers and transporters of goods, and thieves and tricksters. In his winged sandals, he plays the role of dissipating the clouds. Also in Florence, the church of the Santissima Annunziata contains a beautifully painted Annunciation, which is considered to hold magical powers, guarding the locals every time the city was believed to be in great danger. Botticelli also famously depicted scenes from the Pazzi conspiracy in Florence, dated to 1478. The wealthy Pazzi family, with support from Pope Sixtus IV, the king of Naples, and other conspirators, had planned to assassinate the brothers, Guiliano and Lorenzo de Medici, and thus take control of Florence. Through Guiliano succumbed to his stab wounds, Lorenzo escaped, and the Pazzi were swiftly hunted down and brought to justice. Their properties were confiscated and they were erased out of the history, despite their once predominant position in Florentine society. In his depiction of the conspirators on the Piazza della Signoria in Florence, Botticelli's paintings are considered to be visual curses that invoke the malevolent forces of magic. Tourists looking up from the Palazzo Vecchio today can still see the windows on the top floor, that once served as gallows for the conspirators that Botticelli depicted.

La Primavera, by Sandro Botticelli, est. 1470-1480

During the Baroque period, many European universities continued the study of the occult arts. Anthropologists have observed that magical beliefs are still widespread in most developing societies, as well as the traditional cultures of Africa, Asia, Asia, Central and South America, and the Pacific. In his famous book, *The Golden Bough*, Sir James Frazer, a renowned Scottish anthropologist, documents how such beliefs are common in many primitive societies across various continents. One interesting example he cites is that of hunters in certain tribes of New Guinea who use a beetle charm to help them become more successful in spearing turtles or dugongs, a type of manatee. They place small beetles typically found in coconut trees into their spear shafts just behind the spear head. Their "magical belief" is that the spear head will stick well in their prey, similar to how a beetle gets stuck in the human skin when it bites. In his classic book, The Mirror of Magic, the Swiss surrealist Kurt Seligmann expertly describes the history of magic in broad arc that can be traced to Mesopotamia and Persia. He then surveys pre-Middle Age practices like Gnosticism and alchemy, to topics like witchcraft, cabala, and magical arts like the tarot, chiromancy, and astrology. A majority of these practices would fall today under the broad term 'superstition' and most professional magicians will want nothing to do with them, and as we shall see, several of them have gone on to actively debunk these practices. These beliefs and practices also do not lend themselves very well to the scrutiny of scientific observation or experimentation either.

In modern societies, science and technology give us knowledge and control. Despite that, it has been shown by some studies that people whose professions involve a higher level of risk, are more prone to believe in superstitions. Magic might thus be serving the psychological need of providing control and order, and this certainly explains its prominent place in primitive and pre-modern societies. A British archeologist, Ralph Merrifield, was one of the first scholars to make the explicit distinction between religion and magic. In his view, while religion refers to the belief individuals and societies express in supernatural beings or forces, magic is more instrumental in that it is used to bring occult forces under control and therefore influence events and outcomes. Others have argued that these two areas cannot be looked at in isolation, but rather we should think of them as complementary concepts.

The impact of magic and magical thinking can be felt in contemporary culture, and the case of Harry Potter is a standout example. What started as an idea in the fertile imagination of a talented author is now a multibillion-dollar empire. When J.K. Rowling started writing a series of fantasy novels featuring the young wizard, little did she know that her character would soon be part of the global cultural landscape. Since Charlotte's Web in the 1950s, the Harry Potter series of books were the next example of children's books to breaking onto the New York Times bestseller list, reaching the top three positions on the list in 1999. Today, the franchise includes a series of successful books, movies, and even a $500 million theme park, The Wizarding World of Harry Potter, based at Universal Studios in Hollywood. The books and movies in this franchise appeal to kids and grown-ups alike. In his book analyzing the impact of Harry Potter on the popular imagination, Travis Prinzio points out that the stories offer a special type of allure to fans. They don't just represent an escape from the real world, but also contain the power of transformation for both individuals and society at large. Using mythological characters that appeal the imagination, Rowling successfully conveys the power of hopes and aspirations, and the will needed to transform them into action. Like Luke Skywalker, Harry represent the hope to fans of the hero transcending the odds to achieve victory. The series itself is replete with magic and allusions to it. Whether it be the use of specific spells, magical portals to other dimensions, or the acquisition of special powers, the fantasy world of Harry Potter is brought to life by magic.

However, magic and references to it, do not seem to mix well with the hardcore practice of religion today, despite their intertwining in earlier eras. Historically, this is because magic has been associated with the dark side. As a result, the Harry Potter book series by J.K. Rowling and the Hunger Games trilogy by Suzanne Collins are still banned in some religious schools and libraries due to their references to magic and the occult, and the belief that they promote practices like witchcraft, sorcery and Satanism. The Harry Potter series is routinely celebrated in the Banned Books Week run by The American Library Association (ALA) to build awareness that people can and will try to ban books, including children's books. The ALA takes the position that, in the case of children's books, the parents or family should have the final say, rather than an intermediary instituting any kind of global ban. Despite this, the Harry Potter series of books has sold more than 500 million copies worldwide, showing that magic is a potent cultural force.

Several theories have been hypothesized to consider why humans have indulged in magical thinking in the first place. We cannot discount the idea that early humans gained access to magical visions and dimensions through the accidental discovery and use of psychedelic compounds naturally found in some plants. This reinforced the idea of the existence of a "magical plane" which was accessed through these portals, and that was perhaps all encompassing and universal in its character. In his book, Cleansing the Doors of Perception, a nod to the work of Aldous Huxley, the religious scholar Huston Smith suggests that these experiences ended up expanding the perceptions of the early "psychonauts", turning them into the first magicians and shamans, and their newfound knowledge into a vocabulary for understanding the magical and mystical. The noted food writer Michael Pollan recently ventured into this realm through his exploration of the effects of LSD, which is now being introduced in clinical practice, after a prolonged period of being neglected by researchers following the swinging sixties. These entheogens (derived from the "divine within" in Greek), a broad variety of psychoactive substances including LSD, psilocybin and natural compounds like the ones found in ayahuasca are now being explored as treatments for a range of ailments ranging from cancer to chronic alcoholism.

Other more probable explanations include the theory of associative thinking, which posits that humans tend to mistake an imagined connection with a real one. An example of this is the practice by members of the Azande tribe in North Central Africa, who believe that rubbing crocodile teeth on banana plants can lead to a successful harvest of bananas. They associate the curved crocodile teeth with the curvature of the bananas, and having observed that crocodile teeth grow back when they fall, they want to transfer that power back to the banana trees. Sir James Frazer took this idea a step further by suggesting that the entire world-views of some individuals are shaped by a belief in such mimetic or homeopathic principles. This is also referred to as the notion of "like affects like", where two objects once connected are still thought to have a link despite being disconnected later.

With the Industrial Revolution, came the proliferation of clever contraptions and machines that could be designed to evoke seemingly mysterious and magical properties. Not all these contraptions were what they seemed, and some relied on subtle psychological tricks. Among the most famous of these contraptions was the "The Turk", an automated chess player that was thought to be powered by a clock mechanism. Napoleon Bonaparte and

Benjamin Franklin famously played chess games with the Turk, a subject of intense fascination and controversy for several decades. Though it was exhibited by its owners as being an automaton, The Turk was a cleverly designed hoax. Within its confines, it had space to accommodate a skilled human chess player, and over a period of 84 years, it fooled audiences in several countries by concealing skilled chess players who were able to defeat an impressive array of opponents. However, it was famously defeated by François-André Danican Philidor, who is remembered by chess players today for the Philidor Defense (1. e4 e5 2. Nf3 d6). While the Turk was an example of a contraption that wasn't, it turns out that despite the new tools conferred by technology, successful magicians have kept their acts relatively simple and easy to understand, without going completely overboard on props and mechanical contraptions.

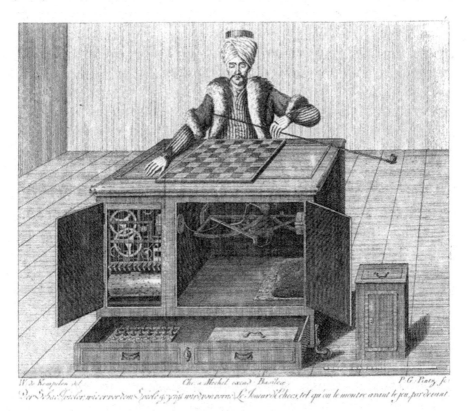

**Copper Engraving of The Turk
(attributed to Kempelen Farkas)**

Becoming A Modern Magician

Our understanding of magic today, especially in advanced industrial and post-industrial societies, is very different from that in primitive or tribal societies, and in particular differs significantly from what was considered part of the magical arts even in the late seventeenth and early eighteenth centuries. The anthropologist Tanya Luhrmann makes the distinction between ritual magic used to achieve instrumental ends, and what we could call entertainment magic or secular magic, whose purpose is to fool an audience that knows it is going to be fooled. We think of magic as a form of entertainment, and magicians as artists or performers who try to create illusions for us that seem like magic. This is a critical difference; believing *in* the magic as a means to achieving an end, versus enjoying something that *seems like* magic, purely for the sake of enjoyment. The other attractions of magic are its capacity to surprise us, its inherent unpredictability, and the strange routes its equally eccentric performers might take to draw us into the spectacle. In this book, the focus is on this type of magic: the skill, art, and practice that can delight and entertain, that can be learned and taught, and is typically performed by stage performers, both at a close-up range in parlor settings or to a larger audience in a big theater.

Developing the skills and expertise needed to be a successful magician takes a different route from other domains like art or music. Accessing specialized and proprietary knowledge of magic is not easy. Most of the magic found through regular channels including in magic stores or online can be thought of as "popular magic". However, maybe this is just a clever misdirection by the pros. To gain entry into a professional circle of magicians, the barriers are a bit higher. To join a group like the International Brotherhood of Magicians, you need to show interest in magic for at least two years prior, as well as gain sponsorship by at least two members. In other words, there is a filtering system in place. Similarly, the Magic Castle in Hollywood or the Magic Circle in London restrict access, and require all applicants to audition. As Loshin, an intellectual property scholar at Yale observes, even Prince Charles, an amateur magician, had to audition to the Circle to be considered for membership. Founded in 1905, the Magic Circle is a premier magic society based in London with an international membership of around 1500. Its Latin motto reads *Indocilis Privita Loqui*, which loosely translates to 'keep your mouth shut'.

Gaining access to "proprietary magic" is even harder to crack, and this can happen only if a critical mass of top practitioners are convinced that they can trust you. Formal training is rare to come by; and most magicians learn mainly through dedicated personal practice and support from informal social networks they are embedded in. Many successful magicians have been fortunate enough to have been nourished through apprenticeships with more established or knowledgeable practitioners, during which they absorb their skills through osmosis, continued formal or informal training, and patient observation and practice. To gain access to such advanced knowledge, they have to establish trusting relationships with the experts, which takes time and effort. There is also no way to subjectively measure magical skills or expertise. A lot of it depends on the audience and its expectations, and whether the magician succeeds in exceeding expectations on one or more dimensions, and the time and setting in which it is done. The skills that a magician will use to perform for his or her peers will be very different from that they may use for a novice audience. As researchers in psychology and business have pointed out, magicians need to be extremely innovative and entrepreneurial in their acquisitions of a diverse body of skills and competencies throughout their careers. They need to be able to quickly classify and organize these skills, develop sophisticated and polished performance routines based on this knowledge, and constantly try to improve and build on their repertoires to create new effects. In other words, they need to develop advanced learning and sense-making techniques, as well as an absorptive capacity that helps them internalize new knowledge rapidly for their own benefit. As essayist Adam Gopnik points out in The New Yorker, there is more to magic than simply knowing how the trick is done. Rather, the "real work" consists of knowing the intricacies of the theatrics, imbibing the accumulated body of knowledge, and the ability to learn from tradition at the hands of expert teachers. While magicians are competitive and eager to impress their peers on the one hand, they are also open to sharing their knowledge and technical skills. By doing so, they not only can improve their own knowledge and skills, but also obtain new ideas for their future performances. This process of creative exchange within the community creates a win-win situation for all its members.

Derived from the Greek word *magos*, magic refers to the member of an elite, learned class. The word has had several meanings ascribed to it, including attraction, delight, fascination, and something alien or different. However, the definition of magic, similar to that of science or religion, has changed over different eras, with the vagaries of time, cultures and social strata. The English writer and bohemian adventurer Aleister Crowley defined *magick* as "the science and art of causing change to occur in conformity with will". This clearly alludes to the control which every magician must have over the outcome of his or her trick, but does not say much about the motivation behind the magic itself. Crowley also believed that rituals helped in separating the magician's ego (in a Freudian sense), and help him or her discover more of the subconscious id. Both art and magic derive from the human need to better understand the world they live in. Even though we live in a secular age driven by science-based advances, instant communications and nearly ubiquitous technologies, magic still holds a spell over our minds and hearts. Despite this, magic and its performance has a tendency to evoke contradictory reactions. As eminent magic scholar and performer Lawrence Hass points out, on the one extreme magic performance ranks low in the spectrum of human pursuits–somewhere between "mime and balloon folding". Yet, on the other end, and especially in the hands of polished performers, we find ourselves drawn to its mystery and wonder, and it has the capacity to transport us to an ecstatic state. Taking this idea further in an entertaining TED Talk, Hass defines magic as "the artful performance of impossible things that generates energy, delight, and wonder". Quite the pithy definition and elevator pitch for magic if there was one. Hass suggests that throughout our lives, we go through the performance of "life magic", and proposes that humans are as much magical animals as rational ones. Therefore, successful magicians not only perform exaggerated versions of the magic we go about performing in our daily lives, but also create experiences that we wish *we* could ourselves perform, whether our desires for this are conscious or still in our subconscious minds.

28

A good magic trick creates a conflict or doubt in our minds between what we have observed, and what we think is possible. The greater the gap between these two points, the greater is our sense of awe or wonder. For that brief moment, we suspend reality, thus getting entranced by the magic itself. Magic is not about suspending belief to accommodate for experiencing conflicting realities. The feeling of contradiction is similar to what we experience when walking on a clear bridge: there is knowledge of safety, but instinctively we find it unsafe. Szabó Gendler says this is a contradiction between belief and what she calls "alief," a more primitive mental state, one that lies outside the realm of belief. Basically, in magic a person does not intellectually believe a trick is real, but emotionally believes that it is real. The better the effect is performed, the greater our emotional belief in its veracity. Clever magicians know that the effect they achieve happens three times, the first time when it is performed, the second in the memory of the spectator, and a third time when they tell a story about it to their friend or acquaintances later. The more spectacular the effect, the more the story will be embellished. Hence, it is important to say and do things that shape the memory and retelling of the effect itself, thus helping to perpetuate the "mythical" status of the magician.

Since it is almost certain that an attentive audience will try hard to explain an illusion, a magician must cancel out all of their ideas on what could really be happening, in order to create a strong belief and conviction. To do this, most magicians incorporate deliberate steps within their routines where they are essentially shooting down each of the observer's theories. In David Copperfield's famous flying routine, he does somersaults, flies through hoops, and flies inside a closed glass box to systematically eliminate any theories the audience could have about how the illusion work. His main objective here is to maximize cognitive dissonance. The brain tries to formulate explanations, and if it cannot find a convincing one, then that very cognitive dissonance that cannot be resolved is the feeling of "magic." For maximum dissonance, a performer must be as close to the crowd as possible, maximizing believability. TV magic is especially hard to believe because one can always suspect camera tricks or video editing. Although the method behind Copperfield's trick can be gleaned by looking at US Patent No.

5,354,238, the choreography and presentation of this illusion are so convincing that one is still willing to suspend one's belief even when armed with this knowledge. Using slightly different methods than David Copperfield, David Blaine pioneered believable TV magic with his show *Street Magic*, which focused on audience reactions to provide evidence of legitimacy. Similarly, the British magician Dynamo and others have carried on this tradition in their TV appearances as well. But TV is still a poor competitor to watching close-up magic live. This is one reason why Penn and Teller like being called up on stage to observe close-up magic, as that is where the rubber meets the road, and true constitution of the magician can be determined. The magician who can demonstrate 'close-up' mastery under the burning gaze of experts and peers thus has every reason to be proud of his or her accomplishment. It is one of the highest rewards in magic.

Due to its uneasy relationship with the worlds of psychics and the supernatural on one hand, and that of hustlers and swindlers on the other, theatrical magic has been all but ignored by art critics and historians. As philosopher Jason Leddington points out, despite its once preeminent status in the world of public entertainment, magic sometimes gets relegated and classified as a sideshow act more suited to kid's parties and the unreality of the Las Vegas strip. However, that might be fast changing with the resurgence of public interest in magic as well as its commercial success. Just as it was a prominent cultural force in Europe and the US in the 19th and early 20th centuries, theatrical magic is well on its way to making a comeback.

Chapter 2: They Made it Happen

The easiest way to attract a crowd is to let it be known that at a given time and a given place someone is going to attempt something that in the event of failure will mean sudden death.

—Harry Houdini

In magic, it takes two or three years for me to create a 5-minute illusion for me to get it to the level I want.

—David Copperfield

Magic in the Popular Culture in the US

Magic occupies a unique place in American culture, one which has historically celebrated confidence, wealth, illusion, and the clever con. Though professional magicians were well established in Europe by the sixteenth century, it took a while before it could make inroads in America. Magic was in fact banned in many early colonies, as the Puritans believed that magic was the work of the devil, and counted as nothing but idle amusements to be avoided. The most extreme example of this attitude were the Salem witch trials in Massachusetts. Considered one of the deadliest witch-hunts in American history, a total of nineteen accused (fourteen women and five men) were found guilty and executed by hanging over a one year span between 1692 and 1693. The list of accused ran over two hundred names. Britain, on the other hand, had experienced something similar nearly a hundred years before the Salem trials. In 1584, Reginald Scot wrote the book *The Discoverie of Witchcraft*, revealing several tricks including the cups and balls routine in what was one of the first textbooks of magic. Interestingly, he was a great supporter of magic, and his motivation in publishing this book was to stop the persecution of magicians by religious leaders during this period. Fortunately for the new colonies, by the time of the American Revolution, the attitudes towards magic had become much more relaxed, resulting in a number of European magicians making their way across to American shores. Magic soon came to recognized for its entertainment value, though its more nefarious side could not be forgotten easily.

In a darkly prophetic novel published on April Fool's day in 1857, The Confidence Man, the writer Herman Melville shows us how the human mind can be skillfully manipulated thanks to its own beliefs, insecurities and fears. The setting is a ride on a riverboat named Fidèle, sailing down the Mississippi from St. Louis and heading to New Orleans, also on April Fool's Day. Just before the boat sets sail, a stranger makes his way up on board. During the journey, he takes on a number of guises to fool and manipulate the passengers. So much so that by the time the journey concludes, the passengers do not know whom to place their trust in anymore. The prototype of the confidence man in popular culture can be traced to a case in New York City in 1849. Samuel Thompson (or Thomas Williams, his alias) would accost strangers on the street, and pretend he knew them from before. Then he would pop the question to his unsuspecting victims, "Do you have confidence in me?". If the answer was in the affirmative, he would ask them to "lend me your watch till tomorrow". Surprisingly, a number of his victims agreed, never to see their valuables again. It is believed that Herman Melville may have seen coverage of the story in the Herald newspaper, as he was living in the city at the time, and it may have influenced his book. While the techniques used by today's magicians may not be so stark or nefarious in intent, they definitely take into account human psychology and our reactions to promises that may seem innocuous on the surface, but may hide ulterior motives. Two successful and big name magicians, David Blaine and Criss Angel, or the Gentleman's Thief, Apollo

Robbins, have skillfully used this knowledge of audience reaction and psychology to stage many of their tricks. Combine this skill with sleight of hand, and you have a formidable magician on the stage or in the street.

Penn and Teller belong to a long lineage of magicians who are constantly trying to bamboozle their audiences, for the purposes of entertainment. Magicians are known for getting their inspiration from diverse fields, and frequently specialize in one or more areas where they can make the best contributions. They are naturally competitive, in a field where one-upmanship is the order of the day. This aspect of magic is depicted well in the aforementioned Hollywood film, The Prestige. The film follows the rivalry between two stage magicians in London at the end of the 19th century. They are both driven to create the best illusion, and outdo one another. Sadly, this competition is carried to the extreme and ends in a tragedy. Starring big Hollywood names like Hugh Jackman, Scarlett Johansson, Michael Caine, Christian Bale, and David Bowie, this movie gave audiences a glimpse of what goes on behind the scenes when it comes to the creative drive and success motivations of magic performers. The movie also alludes to the fierce competition between Thomas Edison and Nikola Tesla, who can be compared to two magicians both performing the same trick. However, only one ends up being memorialized and celebrated (i.e. Edison), and his success may depend more on cunning or luck, rather than pure merit. Similarly, many magicians can perform the same trick, but it may be just one or two who are recognized for their mastery and superlative performance.

The most famous magician who ever lived, Houdini, was fiercely competitive and always sought to outdo his competitors. If his competitor made a horse disappear, he would take on the challenge to make an elephant disappear. This was of course taken to a different extreme by David Copperfield, when he made the Statue of Liberty "vanish". Penn and Teller's humorous take on this was to vanish Elsie the Elephant, and replace her with a what he described as "a common barnyard animal", a chicken. Houdini also went to great lengths to find and develop new ways to achieve his feats, like designing custom lock picks (his tools of the trade). He liked to show off much of his process, which made the tricks seem transparent, fair and believable. He introduced ideas like revealing himself through a glass panel in his Chinese Water Torture Cell, so that the audience could clearly see what was going on. Houdini also marketed his show further by showing his tools to the public and challenging local authorities to lock him up and have him escape their jails. Ahead of his acts, members of the public could examine all the equipment to verify that nothing was "tricked up". Houdini was also one of the pioneers in his use of the media at the time: newspapers, radio, and ingenious techniques of self-promotion. The original "viral marketer", Houdini went to great lengths to ensure that every artefact associated with him, whether it be a photograph, prop, or tool, got widespread viewing and publicity. Today, many magicians are using more modern forms of viral marketing, including YouTube, Facebook or Twitter, but their goal is the same as Houdini–to increase awareness and impact by reaching and communicating with a wide audience of fans and followers. This ability to self-promote is another art form that the best magicians tend to excel at, as we will see in later sections. It is also a skill that is taught, even to the youngest magicians, as the very act of going on stage to present a trick demands a basic knowledge of presentation and promotion.

Penn and Teller themselves have developed a vast repertoire of tricks spanning several categories. These include card tricks, illusions of all kinds, and tricks with specially designed contraptions and effects. They are also polished practitioners of sleight of hand, misdirection, and humor. Penn and Teller specialize in the genre of trickster magic; they are rule-breakers by nature and like to delight and shock the audience with their audacity, dark humor, and cleverness. They made their name as the bad boys of magic, by "performing magic shows for audiences who did not like traditional magic shows". This ability to break convention while constantly try out new genres outside their familiarity zone is a key factor in their ability to innovate as well as remain competitive in a crowded field. In addition to their magical prowess, they are among America's most famous skeptics, and are professed atheists. In fact, they based a whole TV series around this (*Penn and Teller: BS*), which did extremely well and was partly responsible for their focusing on TV as a major platform. They have used their healthy skepticism to inform many of their tricks, often resulting in routines that are entertaining and that defy conventions. Politically, both are libertarians, but have a diverse community of friends and fellow performers with whom they interact on a regular basis. Penn started out performing as a juggler, whereas Teller spent his early days as a teacher. After performing as a pair starting in the early eighties, Penn and Teller slowly gained fame and success, especially after stellar reviews of their Broadway show.

Between 1890 and 1929, Chicago was the epicenter of magic in America, a time referred to as the golden age of magic. This was a time when performers like Houdini, Thurston, and the Chicago native Harry Blackstone Sr. drew crowds to vaudeville houses and major theaters, and mounted enormous tent shows on tours across the country and around the world. In 1893, Chicago became the center of the world's attention thanks to its hosting of the World's Columbian Exposition, also known as the Chicago World's Fair. This was to be an influential social and cultural event that brought together the who's who from around the world, and put Chicago firmly on the map. The spirit of these times is brilliantly captured by Erik Larson in his book *The Devil in the White City: Murder, Magic, and Madness at the Fair That Changed America*. This was a prosperous time for the American economy, and magic performance was firmly established as a major form of entertainment. However, these boom times were not to last too long. After Houdini's death in 1926, and the Great Depression that followed a few years after, the popular tent shows and tours came to a halt in trying economic times. It would take the industrial boom following World War II to bring back quality performers and appreciative audiences to magic shows. Chicago re-established its centrality in the world of magic through the fifties and sixties, with a boom in the unique Chicago style of close-up magic. In parallel, Los Angeles became the center of film production, while New York became the center of radio and Broadway shows. However, by mid-century, there was another slump in magic as popular entertainment. Even the famed director Orson Welles lamented that the field of magic had fallen into decay, a far cry from its successful run in the nineteenth and early twentieth centuries. He believed that all magicians had yielded to using games of perception rather than rely on pure optical and visual effects that the virtuoso magicians of previous generations preferred. He encouraged them to revisit some of the fundamental techniques behind illusions and adapt them to the modern era. Welles himself was known for developing several innovative camera techniques and special effects for his movies, including the *War of the Worlds* and *Citizen Kane*. He also starred in the movie *Black Magic*, in the role of Joseph Balsamo, who was in fact the alleged charlatan, Count Cagliostro, a celebrated figure in his prime. Cagliostro, a self-styled magician and adventurer, was associated with the royal courts of Europe in his role as a psychic, healer and alchemist.

The acceptance of magicians as part of the popular culture underwent a significant change after the widespread diffusion of television. In the 1950s and 60s, there were several entertainers who appeared on American television, whether they be singers or magicians, particularly on platforms like the Ed Sullivan Show, Merv Griffin, Sonny and Cher, etc. A similar dynamic was taking place in the UK as well around this time. This trend continued for the next two decades as performers like Doug Henning, David Copperfield, and Penn and Teller started to gain more prominence, particularly in the seventies and eighties. One interesting observation made by the magician Ryan Hayashi is that a survey of the popular TV shows and movies that predate the mid-eighties, like the A-Team, Knight Rider, MacGyver, Airwolf, The Fall Guy, and others, all have one thing in common. The main protagonist is never the smart guy (or gal). The 'jester' was always portrayed as the smart person but was sadly relegated to minor roles, usually as a comedic prop. By contrast, nearly every popular TV show today celebrates the smart person, be it the latest episode of CSI or Criminal Intent, or a talented magician on *Fool Us*. Hayashi believes that magicians are now the new celebrities, and, as he *coins* it 'smart is the new sexy'. Finally, brains are more important than brawn, representing a radical shift in societal perceptions. The chief protagonist no longer has to rely on courage or guts, or the instinct to punch someone in the face, jump through a window, or drive a car off a ramp. He or she could simply demonstrate what their intellect can do without much pomp and bravado, and still have a devastating effect on the audience. By the nineties, TV was the major platform for performers of all stripes, whether they were professionals or amateurs. This trend has continued into the first two decades of the twenty first century as well. With the proliferation of media options today, the challenge for amateur performers is to pick the right venues to appear on and get the breakthrough they are working for. For established professionals, every new media alternative is a chance to expand into other profitable niches they may have missed, as well as reinforce their core brand and message to a wider audience.

In our contemporary society, magical themes are part of the popular consciousness thanks to the exploits of another popular fictional character, Harry Potter. Blending several genres including fairy tales, myth and legend, school literature, and just plain fantasy, this series has set the standard in bringing magical ideas to the popular discourse. Readers everywhere are familiar with the world of the Muggles, despite the philosophical differences across the pond. While the Harry Potter series has been decried in England as being too strict and conservative, American critics are shocked by the liberal and pagan themes throughout J.K. Rowling's body of work. However, this is not the first series where magic has been the underlying inspiration. Predecessors include the Lord of the Rings series by J.R.R. Tolkien, the Narnia series by C.S. Lewis, and also works by Edith Nesbit and Ursula Le Guin. In the United States, the noted actor and director Neil Patrick Harris, who also served as former President of the Academy of Magical Arts, has debuted a successful series of children's books, The Magic Misfits.

Robert-Houdin to David Blaine:
The Pioneers of Modern Magic

A number of talented magicians have exercised outsized influence on their profession and the industry, and also had major success with the public. It is worth taking a look at their main contributions, as well as the techniques they used to gain a popular following. This list is not exhaustive by any means, but provides a flavor of the variety and unique approaches taken by these well-known practitioners. In particular, my goal is to focus on those magicians who have had the both a significant impact on the profession, and simultaneously enjoyed significant commercial success for a reasonably sustained period of time. The errors of omission here are entirely mine, and it was indeed a difficult task to choose from dozens of contenders to come up with this narrow, subjective list. Also, while reading these profiles, it is important to keep in mind how different the social, economic and cultural contexts were during the heyday of each of these performers, and how the use of mass communication and information technology has completely revolutionized the reach and impact that today's magicians possess.

Considered the originator of the modern style of conjuring, Jean Eugène Robert-Houdin was a trailblazer who revolutionized magic, despite his short performing career that spanned only a decade. Born in 1805, he was the first in a long line of stage magicians to emerge from Europe, and who went on to change the perception of magic in society. The way he got into magic was through a complete accident. As a boy, he had saved up his pocket money to buy a double volume of books on clock making, or horologery. Much to his surprise, upon getting home he discovered that he had ended up with a completely different two-volume set titled Scientific Amusements. Curious, he began reading the books. He got so fascinated that he ended up learning the basic elements of magic from these books, and this became his lifelong obsession. He soon joined an amateur acting group, where he also polished his theatrical skills. Moving to Paris to work in his father's wholesale shop, he could often be found tinkering with mechanical objects and figures. Once again, purely by accident, on one of his walks, he discovered a store that sold magic gear. A gathering place for amateur magicians and aficionados, he soon discovered a community of peers and sponsors who were interested in furthering the craft. He also met Jules de Rovère, an aristocrat who coined the term for sleight of hand used even today, prestidigitation. Another aristocratic patron, Count de l'Escalopier loaned him a princely sum to open up his own theater, the "Théâtre des Soirées Fantastiques", located over the archways in the gardens of the Palais Royal. Attired in a tuxedo with tails, complete with white tie and top hat, Robert-Houdin brought magic off the street and into the theater and the parlor room, and made it dignified and sophisticated, a trend that continued for several decades as magic became part of a civilized entertainment. Soon Robert-Houdin was performing in theaters, with props and mechanical creations he had personally designed. Though slow to take off, once he got some experience under the belt, he was attracting bigger audiences and getting solid reviews.

Among his popular routines was the Ethereal Suspension effect, and The Marvelous Orange Tree. The first involved a levitation where his assistant, his son Emile, would appear to be suspended horizontally in mid-air. The Marvelous Orange tree was more complicated, and relied and his knowledge of constructing automations. In the routine, Robert-Houdin would roll up a handkerchief taken from a spectator into a ball, and place it next to the other items for the trick, an egg, and orange and a lemon. He would then shrink the handkerchief till it appeared to pass through the egg, and similarly shrink the egg till it passed through the lemon, and all of them together into the orange. Next, the orange itself shrunk in his hands until it disappeared, leaving behind a fine powder. This powder was then mixed with alcohol and set on fire. Next, this flame would be placed under a small orange tree filled with green leaves. Magically, the tree would sprout orange blossoms, which soon turned into oranges. The orange at the top of the tree was split open to reveal the missing handkerchief. Two butterflies soon emerged (that were mechanical automatons in reality) and grabbed the handkerchief, unfolding it as they flew up in the air. An even more elaborate version of this trick was shown in the 2006 movie, *The Illusionist*. In retrospect, this was one of the first tricks that relied heavily on technology, and the magician's knowledge to construct elaborate mechanical automatons.

Perhaps his most famous effect was The Light and Heavy Chest. He started by demonstrating a small wooden chest, and would claim that he had found a way to protect it. He would then call upon a small boy from the audience to try and lift the chest, who would then proceed to lift it with ease. Next, he would call upon a larger adult man from the audience (whose strength would be apparent to the audience) to try and repeat the feat. The big man would discover that it was impossible to lift the chest. This ingenious trick used a scientific principle just coming into vogue at the time, Oersted's discovery of electromagnetism. Separating the chest from the attractive force of the magnet under it was too much for even the sturdiest lifter. Robert-Houdin retired from public performances at the age of 48, whereupon he devoted his time to the study of electricity. He was briefly called out of retirement by the Emperor Louis-Napoleon (Napoleon III) to help suppress a rebellion in Algeria. After impressing tribal elders with his performances, the last of which involved catching a bullet between his teeth, he was able to get them to present an offer of peace and swear allegiance to France. This was probably the only time a conjurer was called on to intervene in an armed conflict, and succeeded brilliantly at it. His legacy continues today through his many books and writings, as well a national museum located in his former home which is the only public museum in Europe devoted solely to magic. His fundamental tenet, i.e. the success of the magic performance will be judged solely by its ability to deceive, runs true to this day, and is followed as a guiding principle by all magicians. Through his writings and his performing career, he legitimized magic as a profession and put it on the entertainment map. Throughout his career, he took pride in his work, both as a performer and an inventor.

Born in 1874, Ehrich Weiss was the most successful performer of his generation and perhaps of all time. We know him better as the one and only Harry Houdini. Interestingly, his stage name was inspired by the French magician Jean Eugène Robert-Houdin (1805-1871), who, as we already saw, is credited with bringing magic off the streets and sideshows into elegant indoor settings. Houdini, born in Budapest to a Jewish family, went on to become an American entertainer and a household name. While not the most impressive stage magician, he was considered a master of escapology, a genre of magic which he pioneered and perfected over his career. Known also as the King of Cards, and the King of Handcuffs, he attracted attention on vaudeville in the US. Endowed with a keen athletic prowess since childhood, he gravitated towards acts that required physical endurance and clever illusions. Booked on the Orpheum vaudeville circuit in 1899 after his act with handcuffs got noticed, Houdini was soon performing across the country in the leading vaudeville houses. His next break came in London, where he demonstrated his ability to escape from handcuffs at Scotland Yard. Impressed by this, he was immediately booked for a successful show which soon saw him earning three hundred dollars a week, a minor fortune at the time. Houdini was also a well-known debunker. As President of the Society of American Magicians, he took measures to expose frauds and had a particular distaste for spiritualists, including psychics and mediums. Some famous American spiritualists and mediums included Charles Foster, Henry Slade and the Davenport brothers, all of whom achieved fame on their visits overseas to England, where others like Florence Cook, Mrs. Marshall, Daniel Home and others had already established a field for the practice. The Davenport brothers, for example, had created elaborate methods to fool their audiences, but were exposed as fraudsters during their tours, leading to an eventual decline of the spiritualist movement itself. In his book, *A Magician Among the Spirits*, Houdini documented his efforts at debunking spiritualists and mediums. This led to a rift between him and a famous contemporary of that period, Sir Arthur Conan Doyle, who is remembered today mainly for his Sherlock Holmes series of books. Doyle did not give much credence to Houdini's exposés, being a staunch believer of spiritualism. Strangely enough, Doyle believed that Houdini himself was a spiritualist medium, and was gifted with paranormal abilities. He was simply using debunking to shut out other competitive mediums.

Houdini was also a masterful self-promoter, and went to extreme lengths to build and cement his reputation. Ironically, later in life, he wrote the book *The Unmasking of Robert-Houdin*, as an angry reaction to the refusal of Emile, the son of the widow of Robert-Houdin's to receiving him favorably in Paris in 1901. Houdini then changed the first part of his name to Harry, ostensibly in respect to Harry Kellar, a magician he admired, but more likely an Anglicized version of the name he went by at home, Ehri. Today, while Houdini is a recognized name around the globe, one of his more flamboyant contemporaries who dazzled audiences with his *Levitation of Princess Karnac* trick (made famous by Harry Kellar), and was perhaps a more polished stage magician, Howard Thurston, is scarcely remembered. Jim Steinmeyer, the well-known designer of special effects and illusions, and prolific author of several books on magic, examines the rivalries of this period and provides a fascinating profile of Thurston in his book *The Last Greatest Magician in the World: Howard Thurston versus Houdini & the Battles of the American Wizards*. This goes to show that the winds of recognition and fame are fickle indeed, and success in one generation does not guarantee that others down the road will celebrate one's accomplishments to the same extent. Houdini died tragically at the age of 52. Lecturing at McGill University in Montreal on October 22, 1926, Houdini was relaxing on a couch backstage. A young athlete came up to him and asked if he could really withstand punches to the stomach as he had heard on the grapevine. Before Houdini could prepare himself, the student began punching him with strong blows, and unknown to Houdini, ruptured his appendix. He died shortly after on Halloween day, October 31st, from complications of that injury.

Another highly respected magician and mentor to several famous performers was the Canadian expert on close-up magic, Dai Vernon. Vernon, born in 1894, lived for nearly a century and not only saw tremendous changes in the world of magic during his lifetime, till his death in 1992, but also presided over several of them in the world of close-up magic. In the tradition of Houdini, David Verner changed both his first and last names, due to curious circumstances. He adopted Dai instead of David, as a Canadian newspaper once misspelled his first name (conveniently, Dai was the Welsh name for David). Later, he adopted Vernon instead of Verner as people used to confused his name with that of a popular ice skating pair at the time. Vernon's introduction to magic came at a very young age. Introduced to card tricks through the book originally titled *Artifice, Ruse and Subterfuge at the Card Table: A Treatise on the Science and Art of Manipulating Cards*, by S.W. Erdnase, which he mastered using miniature cards, Vernon's mastery of close-up magic was matched by his magnetic personality and his ability to attract magicians from far and wide. This abstruse book, later released as *The Expert at the Card Table*, became one of the classics of card magic. The great magician Harry Houdini had insisted that he could decipher any trick if it was repeated thrice to him. One of Vernon's early accomplishments was in fooling Harry Houdini with his Ambitious Card routine, despite repeating the trick for him seven times in a row. After that successful encounter, Vernon publicized himself using the title *The Man Who Fooled Harry Houdini*. Interestingly, the key to this ruse was his use of multiple methods to achieve the same effect. Even the great physicist and

Nobel Laureate Richard Feynman, would could decipher most magic effects presented to him after some thought, would be baffled by tricks that used multiple methods to achieve the same effect. Most of all, Dai Vernon evokes great admiration among magicians for his ability to teach and mentor qualified aspirants, which is what he did with great success during his days at the Magic Castle. Perhaps the most evocative description of his presence there comes from the magician Nick Lewin, which is reproduced below:

> "Upon entering the Castle, once you had passed through the sliding bookcase, the first thing most magicians would do was turn their gaze to the left and see if Dai Vernon was in his regular seat on the little couch in front of the Close-Up Gallery. Most nights would find him holding court there, with a cigar in one hand, a deck of cards in the other, and a snifter of brandy on the table in front of him. Seated around "The Professor" would be a crowd of the very best of the current crop of Young Turks hanging on his every word. They were waiting for him to casually impart the "moves" and gems of card handling in person that had escaped being immortalized in his written work. They were seldom disappointed."

Vernon was an amateur performer until he was in his forties. Vernon achieved his reputation thanks to his expertise with and contributions to close up magic, especially with objects like cards and coins. He discovered and perfected a lot of his card tricks after traveling extensively all over the country, in a bid to discover and document the techniques used by sleight-of-hand artists and card cheats. In that sense, he was both a connoisseur and historian of close-up magic. He was also the originator of the standard "cups and balls" routine, which is a stock in trade for most close-up magicians today. Though Vernon rarely held a steady job for most of his early life, he ended up spending his last thirty years as the Magician-in-Residence and star attraction at The Magic Castle in Los Angeles, where he mentored some top magicians including Doug Henning and Ricky Jay, among others. He wrote a series of books that are considered the gold standard for close up magicians, including *Dai Vernon's Book of Magic*, and *Inner Secrets of Card Magic*. During his career, he pioneered several card effects, including Cutting the Aces, Twisting the Aces, Jumping Jacks, The Travelers, Stars of Magic, and many others. These are part of the standard syllabus for any self-respecting card magician today. After his death in 1992, his ashes were interred at the Magic Castle, his longest residency and home.

It would be remiss not to mention one of Vernon's illustrious students, Ricky Jay, who, while not a major big show entertainer, had an enormous influence on fellow magicians interested in close-up magic, as well as being one of the most knowledgeable historians and prolific collectors the world of magic has ever seen. Jay, who passed away recently in November 2018, was gifted sleight of hand magician, an accomplished author, a fount of magic knowledge and arcana, as well as an accomplished actor with an extended filmography and successful appearances on TV, Broadway and blockbuster Hollywood movies. Jay appeared in several Hollywood films like Tomorrow Never Dies, Boogie Nights, and TV shows like The X-Files and Deadwood. During his lifetime, Jay was hopelessly addicted to amassing an eclectic collection of magic and vaudeville artifacts, including rare books and manuscripts, art, props, and frequently found himself financially stretched while supporting his collector habits. In a fascinating profile of Ricky Jay in the New Yorker, Mark Singer reveals the range and diversity of his talent, as well as his quirky and charismatic personality. One of his trademark acts was demonstrating the use of playing cards as projectiles, which he would aim at his favorite stage target, a watermelon. He held the Guinness world record for card throwing in 1976, having thrown a card 190 ft. at 90 miles per hour (the current record is 216 feet). He also wrote a satirical book based on this arcane skill, appropriately titled 'Cards as Weapons'. His consulting firm, Deceptive Practices, gave frequent advice to Hollywood producers and directors, especially when it came to designing unusual props or illusions to be used in movies. His was a consultant for well received movies like Ocean's Thirteen, The Illusionist, The Prestige and Mission: Impossible–Rogue Nation. A documentary about his life "Deceptive Practice: The Mysteries and Mentors of Ricky Jay," offers viewers insights into this creative 'magician of magicians', including his many mentors and influences like Dai Vernon, Charlie Miller, Al Flosso, Cardini, Slydini, Francis Carlyle, and his own grandfather, Max Katz. His book about the German performer Matthias Buchinger is considered to be a classic, and now a hard to find collector's item. It's curious title reads–'Matthias Buchinger "The Greatest German Living": By Ricky Jay Whose Peregrinations in Search of the "Little Man of Nuremberg" are Herein Revealed'. Buchinger (1674-1740), a German magician and calligrapher born without hands or feet, went on to astonish his contemporaries with his magic tricks, performances that demonstrated his physical dexterity, his talent at micrography, and his ability to invent and play several musical instruments. And, as Jay liked to remind his audiences, he had four wives and also fathered fourteen children. He probably ranks the highest in the array of strange and unique individuals that Ricky Jay studied and documented over his lifetime. In 2016, the Metropolitan Museum in New York held a commemorative show featuring Buchinger's drawings from Jay's collection titled *Wordplay: Matthias Buchinger's Drawings from the Collection of Ricky Jay*.

Self Portrait by Matthias Buchinger
(This drawing is so intricate that when examined under a microscope, the curls of his hair reveal seven inscribed biblical psalms and the Lord's Prayer. And it was made by an artist who was born without arms and legs.)

The next magician on our list, Doug Henning, is credited with creating some of the most famous and popular illusions in magic. A prolific performer in the 70's and early 80's, Henning made his mark on Broadway and also appeared extensively on television. He had the ability to amaze audiences with illusions that had never been seen before: disappearing assistants, levitation tricks, and impossible escapes. He combined this with a breezy and colorful style of performance. His version of "Metamorphosis" is an iconic act. An illusion inspired by his idol Harry Houdini, the act is both simple and stunning. After being handcuffed and tied in a sack, his assistant is put in a chest which is then padlocked. Henning proceeds to stand atop the chest and counts to three. The next thing you know, they have exchanged places, with his assistant now on top of the chest, while Henning is in the chest, handcuffed and locked. Henning performed this act much faster than his idol Houdini. He also revived Houdini's Chinese Water Torture illusion, for which he had to prepare for nearly seven months. NBC signed him on and Henning's first World of Magic special aired on December 26, 1975. On the show, Henning successfully performed the water torture illusion, though he did not break Houdini's time record. His unique Magic Show musical on Broadway is credited with ushering in a golden age of magic, by taking traditional routines into the realm of mass media and entertainment. Magic had entered a time where spectacle would be cherished and entertainment value would be rewarded handsomely. He ended up performing the Chinese Water Torture Illusion throughout his career. Originally debuted in 1913, in this act he had to escape from a locked steel and glass cabinet while being suspended upside down, and having to hold his breath for more than three minutes. Popular tricks like 'Metamorphosis,' have been adapted and improved on by other magicians. The husband-wife team of the Pendragons performed it with great skill and it became their signature performance; more recently, performers like Criss Angel, and the French magician Frederic Clement have performed some of the fastest versions known.

Henning is credited with reviving the magic industry which was facing a significant slump in the seventies. His main contribution was in changing magic performance from the traditional and stuffy tuxedo and bowtie approach to a free-flowing rock and roll style, and incorporating music, comedy and performance art. His soon earned a Tony award for a long running show on Broadway titled *The Magic Show,* which debuted in 1974. During this time, he also performed regularly in Lake Tahoe and Las Vegas. Attired in tie-dye T-shirts, jeans, and flashy jumpsuits, he cut a colorful figure on and off stage. Between breaks, he would practice meditation and yoga. He was frequently spotted in magic shops and bookstores around the country, where he would casually chat with fans and autograph their books. Here was a magician who loved his trade with every fiber of his being. Tragically, Henning died at the age of 52 from liver cancer, having lived as long as Harry Houdini. Just like they do with Houdini, magicians everywhere still hold him in awe for his breakthrough innovations and daring style, and Henning is considered one of the true pioneers of modern magical performance. Henning realized he was breaking convention by choosing to work in an industry that was in a deep slump, and faced an uncertain future. He pointed out his predicament in a popular quote, "'When I was in college, being a magician was not the classiest thing to be. It was like being a folk singer before Bob Dylan." In the early eighties, he had another successful run at Broadway with his show *Merlin*, which earned another five Tony nominations. He is also remembered for the biography he co-wrote, titled *Houdini: His Legend and His Magic*. Towards the end of his life, he sold many of his illusions to David Copperfield, and retreated to his newfound interest in transcendental meditation.

Lance Burton was another influential and commercially successful magician who performed nearly 15,000 shows in Las Vegas over his 31-year career. Through much of it all, he kept up a grueling schedule of three shows a day, seven days a week. He became the youngest magician and the First American to win the "Grand Prix" prize at the FISM competition in Switzerland, in 1982. In 1996, he started performing in the custom designed Lance Burton Theater at the Monte Carlo Resort in Las Vegas. His show earned him an estimated $110 million, and came to be rated as the most family friendly magic show. Besides his primary residence at the Monte Carlo Resort, Burton made numerous appearances on the Tonight Show with Johnny Carson, Jay Leno, and also Craig Ferguson;

and cameos in TV specials and series. In 1999, he had a narrow escape while staging an illusion for a "Top Secret" special he was filming. As part of the act, he appeared to escape just in time from the path of "The Desperado", one of the fastest and tallest roller coasters in the United States. Located at the Buffalo Bill's Hotel and Casino in Primm, Nevada, the Desperado is a hyper coaster which boasts 225-foot drop down a 55-degree descent on the first hill, followed by a 155 drop on the second. The second drop is rated at 4G's, higher than the 3.5G's the astronauts feel at takeoff. In his TV appearance, Burton miscalculated the speed of the coaster and avoided a certain collision with less than a tenth of a second to spare. This escape is still debated among members of the Magic Cafe, an online forum bringing together magicians and magic enthusiasts, with some ascribing it to skillful TV editing. Known for his persistence and tenacity, Burton constantly tested the effectiveness of his performances by evaluating the audience response to every routine. His operating philosophy was that any aspiring magician could steadily improve their craft through repeated practice, hypothesis formulation, experimentation, and evaluation. Indeed, this lesson could be applied by any manager or entrepreneur as well. Burton set the bar for magic performance in Las Vegas with his tenacity, persistence and dedication to his chosen profession. One of the popular tricks he developed, consists of a sword fight where he is challenged by a masked intruder on stage. Burton takes on the swordfight challenge, and then hides under a tablecloth, whereupon the challenger stabs him. When he pulls the tablecloth off, Burton has vanished. The intruder takes off his mask, and it is revealed to be Burton. Upon his retirement, Burton gave Criss Angel permission to continue staging the sword fight.

David Copperfield, the next in the line of blockbuster magicians, is considered to be the most successful magician and solo entertainer in history. As of 2018, he had grossed over $4 billion in ticket sales, with over 33 million tickets sold, and his shows at the MGM have sold out for 13 years straight. He adopted his stage name after watching the synonymous play by Charles Dickens (his given name being David Seth Kotkin). Throughout his career, he has specialized in developing and performing spectacular high-octane acts. Among his feats outdoors: making the Statue of Liberty "vanish" and reappear, levitating over the Grand Canyon, walking through the Great Wall of China, and escaping from Alcatraz. During his stage performances, his repertoire is varied, with a number of disappearances, getting cut in half, and levitation routines. The climax of these shows is his artistic and gravity defying Peter Pan routine, where he effortlessly floats and flies around the stage. As one critic put it, "he could probably retire just by selling his secrets to future productions of Peter Pan". He holds eleven Guiness records, including that for most tickets sold worldwide by a solo entertainer, and the largest illusion ever staged. One major factor of his longevity is his legion of diehard fans (read: loyal and repeat customers), many of whom are now bringing their kids and grandkids to his shows. Interestingly, Copperfield's major influences early in life were not magicians. Rather, he admired stars like Gene Kelly, Fred Astaire and Frank Sinatra, and studied the work of film directors like Alfred Hitchcock, Orson Welles and Frank Capra. Obviously, this had a major influence on his style of performance, whose foundations are storytelling, choreography and theater. In addition to his successful businesses, Copperfield also owns two museums dedicated to preserving magic artefacts: The International Museum and Library of the Conjuring Arts, and the Mulholland Library of Conjuring and the Allied Arts. He purchased the latter in 1991, and among other items, it houses several historically significant props and artefacts, including automata created by Robert-Houdin, Houdini's Water Torture Cabinet and Metamorphosis Trunk, and Orson Welles' Buzz Saw illusion.

David Blaine is credited with the next major breakthrough in magic performance. By turning the camera to the audience and capturing audience reactions (or shock) in detail, he turned the tables on street and close-up magic performance. His TV special *Street Magic*, has been credited by Penn Jillette as "the biggest breakthrough (in television magic) done in our lifetime". Using guerilla tactics to perform sleight of hand tricks on the street, he graduated to close up magic performed in the company of assorted celebrities and hangers-on. While the show offers a more gritty, close-up perspective, it is still a TV show with its own rituals of staging, camera angles, and editing. Blaine's breakthrough is to make the viewer feel that he or she is right next to him as he performs the tricks; and the impromptu street audience in the shows serve as proxies for viewers watching the show at home. The participants in some of these tricks include an esoteric cast of characters: Kanye West, young men hanging out at a Bronx housing project, Stephen Hawking, Harrison Ford, George W. Bush and Woody Allen. Blaine is not afraid of either performing tricks which test the limits of his own endurance, or cause nauseating effects on his audience, or both. In his ABC special *Beyond Magic*, he displays his special brand of close-up magic, whether it is regurgitating live frogs into champagne flutes held by his celebrity friends Steph Curry, Drake and Dave Chappelle; or eating a wine glass in front of Don Cheadle and Arnold Schwarzenegger. Through his pioneering approach, Blaine revolutionized the concept of close-up magic, taking the audience interaction and the capturing of audience reactions to an entirely new level.

Blaine's other claim to fame is in performing public endurance feats; interestingly, many of them were performed within blocks of each other in New York City over a span of a decade or more. In his 'Buried Alive' feat, he entered a three-ton water filled tank with around six inches of headroom. Staged at Trump Place on the Upper West Side, he stayed in the tank for seven days. More than 75,000 witnessed the feat during the week. In his next endurance performance, he was 'Frozen in Ice' at Times Square in Manhattan. Encased in a huge block of ice, he spent over 63 hours (3 days). He was finally pulled out after the ice was sawed off; medics feared he would go into shock after such prolonged exposure to cold. He suffered a concussion when he jumped on to a set of boxes in his next performance; this was after he had stood on a hundred-foot high pillar at Bryant Park for 35 hours. Even more extreme, he moved on to London in 2003, where he was suspended thirty feet in the air in a transparent case for 44 days. His only nourishment during this time was four and half liters of water each day. At the end of the ordeal, he lost nearly a quarter of his body weight. He also had to endure taunts like being teased with a hamburger flown outside his case by a remote-controlled helicopter. He considers it to be his best feat. One of his memories from the event is the sweet taste of water every time he drank it for the first four weeks.

This was in stark contrast to what he felt thereafter, when his organ walls were soon being digested slowly, and even water felt sulfurous. During that feat, he was truly pushing the limits and suffered liver and kidney damage. His next personal challenge was to break the underwater static apnea breath-holding record, which didn't go well after he had to be pulled out at 7 minutes. He did end up breaking the record for holding his breath long enough (with an oxygen assist beforehand). Blaine has thus carved out a niche for himself in this space through his audacious and death defying acts. Like Houdini before him, Blaine is also the master of self-promotion. Even before the start date of many of his stunts, Blaine is known to spend extraordinary effort in generating pre-launch publicity, in some cases, as much as a year in advance. On the launch date, he turns his stunt into spectacles, with continued media coverage, live feeds, and now, a significant social media presence. During and after his feats, he manages to keep up a continued presence on media, through interviews, stories, and planned press coverage. In effect, media scholars contend that through the preparation, execution and post-feat discussion, Blaine is acting out the fear of the rapt audience, putting it on full display, and thus providing and providing a valuable therapeutic exercise through his performance. The medium of reality TV adds a sense of spontaneity and opens up the possibility of the unexpected. He could thus be labeled a modern day 'TV Shaman'. Contrary to traditional performances where the magician does all the talking and the audience watches in silence, Blaine, in many of his stunts, is completely silent, immobile and vulnerable, while the tuned-in audience openly and vociferously voice their fears, insecurities, doubts, and opinions about what they are watching. In his close-up magic based heavily on audience interaction and reaction, Blaine relies on triggering shock and revulsion as much as fine sleight of hand for the tricks to work. In a recent appearance on Jimmy Fallon, Blaine was able to shock the audience after first having his mouth sewn shut with a thread and needle. Fallon had the privilege of tying the ends of the string around his pierced lips. The actress Priyanka Chopra, who had earlier selected a playing card, was also stunned when his lips were unsealed. There, he not only revealed the correct card and, but to the shock of the audience–a live frog that he spat out into a glass of water. Blaine has repeated this trick in other venues, and rarely fails to elicit genuine surprise, shock and disgust from his close-up audience. In that sense, Blaine can be considered one of the "shock jocks" of contemporary magic.

In parallel with David Blaine, another performer who created a niche for himself using street stunts using bystanders (real or staged), innovative video splicing, and extreme special effects, is Criss Angel. Achieving his fame (and some would say notoriety) through his TV series, Mindfreak, which aired from 2005 to 2010, he has gone on to produce and star in numerous long running shows on the Las Vegas strip. His rock star persona is more than an act, as he was formerly the lead singer in his industrial band, Angeldust, and has produced five albums between 1998 and 2003. His TV show is known for its homemade quality with lowbrow aesthetics, but Angel is fully aware and in control of every angle and effect being used. Criss Angel performs his signature show Mindfreak! at Planet Hollywood in Las Vegas, and has previously starred in record breaking shows like *Criss Angel BeLIEve*, as well as *Magicjam* and *Mindfreak LIVE!*. Relying on special effects including like pyrotechnics, lasers, and explosions, his show is meant to entertain on a dramatic scale, complementing his provocative and occasionally dark persona. Like Blaine, Angel has also pursued extreme endurance feats and holds the world record for the longest time submerged under water, and the longest body suspension timed at 5 hours and 42 minutes, among others. He also performed the *Metamorphosis* illusion in the fastest time recorded, at less than one second. In 2010, he earned the Guinness world record for making 100 people 'disappear' in an illusion at the Luxor in Las Vegas. Angel is also a self-confessed workaholic and perfectionist. He routinely spends up to 18 hours a day at work, and he believes that it is necessary especially now that he is a top performer. One of his claims to fame is that he has been aired on primetime TV more than all the other top magicians combined. This includes the formidable list of Houdini, Copperfield, Siegfried and Roy, Doug Henning, and Penn and Teller. He views himself as an artist first and foremost, and one who performs magic and illusions with the intention of provoking audience emotions. He has used that skill to particular effect when it comes to convincing TV audiences, and exploiting the medium's advantages to bring shock and awe into our living rooms.

One of the most influential magicians living today is Johnny Thompson, universally recognized as a major influence in the field of performance magic, in his varied roles as a virtuoso performer, educator, consultant, and mentor. In this last role, he has mentored many of the top magicians including Penn and Teller, Criss Angel, Mat Franco and Lance Burton. John Thompson, a native of Chicago, began his entertainment career playing harmonica in the group Harmonicats in 1951, and later pioneered his own brand of comedy magic. Inspired by a movie that he watched in 1942-1943 about a Mississippi riverboat gambler, he was tempted to follow a career as a card shark, but ended up performing close-up magic. With his wife and assistant Pamela Hayes, he appeared in the role of The Great Tomsoni, a slapstick magic act which features Thompson as a well-appointed but bumbling magician who speaks with a thick Polish accent, while his indifferent gum-chewing assistant Pam barely cooperates during the routines. Taylor Martin, a co-producer of the Indianapolis Winter Magic Festival, has called Thompson the world's greatest all-round magician. This is a well-deserved title given that Thompson's career has covered everything from illusions, mentalism, bar magic, and dove and silk magic, to working with some of the world's top magicians as a consultant. In fact, he considers himself a "General Practitioner" of magic. In his role as consultant, he serves as the backstage arbiter on *Penn and Teller: Fool Us*. In his honor, Penn and Teller performed their version of The Great Tomsoni and Co., on their show, with Teller appearing as Tomsoni. Jamy Ian Swiss, the author of a respected collection of essays on the craft of magic, titled *Shattering Illusions*, *Devious Standards* and *Preserving Mystery*, has produced a 600 page, two volume set titled *The Magic of Johnny Thompson*, which covers the entire range of Thompson's tricks in meticulous detail. This limited edition set also carried the original signatures of both John Thompson and The Great Tomsoni. Thompson is also a fixture on the magic scene in Las Vegas, having worked there for several decades, and being at the forefront of several acts from their inception to eventual success. Swiss, who is a well-known historian and magician, considers Cardini and Channing Pollock to be the two most influential magicians of the twentieth century. Cardini specialized in sleight-of-hand tricks and was a major influence to many magicians who followed in his path, including Ricky Jay and others. Pollock was a charismatic entertainer as well as a former professor at the University of California, Berkeley, where he lectured on the art of deception. Like Thompson, they left behind a generous legacy through their innovations and teachings.

It is indeed difficult to compare or rank magicians from different eras and especially without objective measures, or taking into account the prevailing market trends. Among the newer magicians competing to make their mark in this august pantheon are names like Dynamo, Derren Brown, Shin Lim (who performs with the Illusionists), and Ryan Hayashi. Dynamo and Brown in particular are well established, both in the UK as well as Las Vegas, and already rank among the most successful in terms of their career earnings. We will discuss some of their recent achievements and examine the potential of their sustained and large-scale commercial success in future sections.

Misdirection, Sleight of Hand, and the link to Neuroscience

"Neuroscientists are novices at deception. Magicians have done controlled testing in human perception for thousands of years."
—Teller

Magic is an art form where you lie and tell people you are lying.
—Teller

While both magicians and neuroscientists are interested in the workings of the brain, their approaches are different: while the former are interested in fooling the brain by exploiting its foibles, the latter are concerned with following and understanding the brain as it processes information, and makes critical inferences or decisions, thus trying to comprehend this marvelous and complex organ. It is still not clear who has the upper hand here in terms of understanding the brain, given that magicians have been at it for centuries. It is clear that magicians are experts at illusions of all kinds through these years of experimentation, and this includes illusions still not analyzed or understood by science. Consider one of John Thompson's routines, in which he promises to change a woman's dress from white to red. He turns on a red stage light, as a joke, but once the light turns back to white, the woman is wearing a red dress. Thompson relies on a series of subtle manipulations to hide the illusion. First, the woman is wearing a very tight dress, suggesting that nothing could be worn underneath it. Second, the woman is attractive, which focuses eyes on her rather than the stage floor, and accustoms the audience's eyes to the light of the stage. When the light dims and brightens again in white, the audience cannot see the dress being ripped off by invisible cables. Also, the fact that the actual trick is performed only when the audience thinks it is over tricks them into lowering their guard. This classic example of a cognitive illusions relies on the concept of "misdirection," which is diverting the audience's attention away from one element of a trick to another, unimportant element. Misdirection takes two forms, overt and covert, and two dimensions, space and time. Misdirection has its cognitive base in inattentional blindness (failing to notice an object in plain sight) and change blindness (failing to notice that something has changed). Attention manipulation can further be broken up into two categories, top-down and bottom-up attention control. In top-down control, the magician directs the spectator to look at something, whereas in bottom-up control the spectator's attention shifts of their own accord. This is complemented by the use of body language or humor to create social misdirection, as well as forms of memory illusions that enable the performer to implant false or altered memories in spectators. They can also employ illusory correlations that convince the audience that a cause and effect relationship exists where there is none.

Techniques like misdirection and the manipulation of attention, commonly used by magicians for a very long period of time, are now being studied closely by neuroscientists to understand how the brain constructs a subjective reality based on imperfect information. Scientists, like magicians, have long known that the brain processes as little information as possible, but makes inferences based on prior assumptions. The German physicist Hermann von Helmholtz, inventor of the ophthalmoscope and the pre-eminent expert of his time in physiology and optics, argued more than a hundred years ago that the eye is a poor gatherer of information. In order to compensate, the brain steps in to make unconscious inferences of what we see around us. Previous illusion researchers believed that illusions were critical failures of brain processes. Rather, they are the byproduct of efficient processing shortcuts that our brain uses to quickly analyze a scenario. Much of our perception of the world is not accurate, but serves its purpose of keeping us alive. Thus, we make a lot of decisions based on subjective interpretations rather than objective facts, and magicians skillfully leverage this fact using techniques like misdirection. The audience thus sees one thing but they are internalizing it as what the magician wants them to subjectively interpret. A good example of this is the Miser's Dream trick performed to great effect by Teller, and part of the repertoire of most parlor magicians. It is also an easy one to perform with some practice and a great way to entertain kids. Teller seemingly fetches coins one after the other from thin air, which he then proceeds to drop into a metal bucket. Every time a coin drops in, we hear a satisfying clink, and the brain interprets this as the reality (coin plucked from air and dropped into bucket). What is unknown to the audience is that it is the same coin he is plucking every single time, while his other hand is releasing previously hidden coins into the bucket in perfect synchrony. All Teller has to do is to ensure that he palms the original coin while we are thus misdirected, and magically produce it again as many times as he likes. Other entertaining versions of this trick include the performances by Jeff McBride and Al Flosso. In a revealing letter to a fan and aspiring magician, Teller describes how he worked on the delivery of the Miser's Dream effect for nearly eight years, before being completely satisfied. His advice to the young magician was to be sparing in divulging too much of the general plot of the trick, but at the same time holding the audience's attention. This engages the audience to try and figure out what is going on, even as they are fed incrementally more information by the performer. After some misdirection, and a false ending, go in a completely different direction for the big finish. Of course, these ideas can be applied to any trick, but the key takeaway is that a simple looking effect can take time to mature and get fully polished even in the hands of the expert performer.

Researchers in psychology, and increasingly in neuroscience, are exploring the various dimensions of magic in order to study issues in human perception and cognition. As early as 1894, psychologists like Binet were studying magicians to understand how sleight of hand really worked. Binet, who is known for his development of the IQ test, using the technique of stop-action photography to investigate how magician's sleight-of-hand techniques. By today's standards this would be considered a primitive measurement technique, but it was sufficient for Binet to determine some of the underlying methods. Over the years, techniques like eye tracking have been used to understand how subjects follow a performance, and how their attention is diverted deliberately by magicians. Today, neuroscientists are using sophisticated tools like fMRI to investigate how the brain reacts to various stimuli, including misdirection. fMRI, or functional magnetic resonance imaging requires the subject to lie down inside a brain scanner, while observing stimuli projected on a screen. The scanner records brain activity in real time during this exercise, and this can then be analyzed for patterns, like understanding which parts of the brain get activated. Richard Gregory, the late British psychologist and perception scientist, had a much more radical explanation of illusions and how they are perceived. His view was that illusions were instances where our sensory systems broke down. However, more recent researchers like Macknik, et al have argued that illusions are the normal scheme of things rather than the exceptions. They are a method by which the brain takes shortcuts, providing us with just the minimal amount of information needed to survive, while using its processing power for other tasks that also require attention. The study of cognition and its limitations has continued, including in the important field of economics. The path-breaking work of Daniel Kahneman glaringly exposed the assumption of rational behavior in decision-making by human beings. Human decision making, it turned out, was driven by flaws and emotions as much as it was by rational thinking. When presented with novel information, our decision making and problem solving processes follow two complementary systems or pathways. This is the famous dual-process model proposed by the Nobel Prize winning economist Kahneman. The first systematic way we approach the problem is our reliance on intuition and unconscious reasoning, that is completely automatic and does not use the full cognitive capacity of the brain. The second is when our brain power kicks in and we follow a more analytical process for reasoning. This process tends to be very controlled and conscious, and tends to be slower and also relies on more brain power or cognitive resources. When we witness a skilled magician perform a complicated routine, we are relying primarily on the first method of problem solving, which is faster but much more prone to error and cognitive biases. One reason our failure in correctly getting the answer is that we are substituting the problem we saw with a simpler (but completely different) problem to which we can come up with a faster answer. As Kuhn and others have proposed in an application of this concept to magic, this could indeed explain why we are so easily fooled by simple sleight-of-hand tricks. The real trick being played on us is that magician is not giving us access to our full cognitive capabilities to understand what we are seeing, and thus tricking our brains to take the easy way out.

Similarly, another Nobel Laureate, Herbert Simon, who elucidated the theory of bounded rationality, showed how we adopt a satisficing behavior when it comes to our decisions, thus not using our entire capacities for using information. His theory argues that our rationality is limited by the information we possess, the amount of time available to make the decision, and the cognitive limitations of our minds. When we carry these ideas over from individual to group behavior, it becomes easy to see that our decisions can be influenced significantly by artists who know how to manipulate the very foundations of our attention and cognition. In order to gain more insight into this phenomenon, I revisited the work of one of my colleagues who has examined this tendency of humans to seek simple explanation for events and the ability of others (or external events) to manipulate this worldview. Nassim Nicholas Taleb, a former trader turned academic, is known for his popular series of books starting with the *Black Swan: The Impact of the Highly Improbable*. In his work, he explains that when presented with new and unfamiliar information, we are already handicapped in our abilities to make proper inferences. This may be due to our limited range of expertise in a very narrow area, or inaccurate extrapolation of our current problem-solving abilities to a new domain. He argues that narrow expertise has severe limitations, as we often miss the forest for the trees.

Magicians are artists of attention and awareness, and are clever users of both visual and cognitive illusions. Cognitive illusions involve attention, memory, and causal inference. Neuroscientists are trying to adapt magic in order to further explore cognitive functions by studying the effects of specific magical techniques. For example, they believe that focus manipulation tricks can help reduce distraction during Alzheimer's therapy. In magic, diverting attention is called "misdirection," and it has two forms, overt and covert. Overt misdirection involves redirecting the audience's gaze to a distraction. Covert misdirection is subtle and does not require a person to redirect their gaze. Two examples are change blindness and inattentional blindness, which are, respectively, when a person fails to compare pre-change and post-change memories and when a person fails to realize an object in plain sight, usually due to a preoccupation or illusion. In either case, diversion of audience attention needs to be achieved irrespective of the means. The three commonly used misdirection techniques involve a. occupying a person with a task to keep them distracted, b. baiting people into thinking a solution is obvious, causing them to stop looking for the real solution, or c. redoing a trick and changing the method, timing, or result to throw peoples guesses off. On the issue of social misdirection (using social cues to direct attention, e.g. glancing), recent studies have found that the impact of such misdirection is actually less than thought. But some follow up studies suggest that it has a variable efficacy based on whether a spectator is already deceived or undeceived by an act. In one interesting experiment, a comparison was made between two groups witnessing a "cups and balls" trick on a video clip, with a number of different parameters meant to test the impact of social misdirection. The findings were that deception was correlated with increased glances at the magician's face, indicative of a correlation between deception and social misdirection. However, as there were some undeceived individuals who glanced at the magician's face, there may still be factors such as type of social attention that impact the potency of social misdirection. In a talk at the Magic of Consciousness Symposium held in 2007, Teller demonstrates how the intensity of intention projected by the magician can be sufficient to misdirect the audience. This intention can be conveyed either by physical movements, verbal messaging, or a combination thereof, and experienced magicians can thus exploit the misdirection to successfully undertake the real objective of the trick.

In a study of the disappearing cigarette trick, psychologists discovered that it made no difference where the spectators were looking when the cigarette disappeared. In a study of the "vanishing-ball illusion," psychologists found that after the ball was thrown and caught a few times and then pretended to be thrown, spectators believed it to have vanished because the magician's pretending to track the ball with his eyes and making a throwing hand motion were what the spectators focused on, instead of whether the ball was actually in the air. It was found that the neurons that detect actual motion and the neurons that detect implied motion are the same, explaining why the audience feels that they see the ball actually go up when it did not. Thus, our brain is painting its own version of reality based on quickly assimilating a pattern that it has observed, though the empirical data does not support its conclusion. It is a classic instance of extrapolation based on extremely limited but convincing data.

In other cognitive tricks, magicians follow up their tricks with challenges to the audience to reveal the secret and "reconstruct" the trick, and with every guess that is proven wrong the spectator's belief in the trick becomes more concrete (thus creating cognitive dissonance). "Informing the motion" is the term used to describe disguising sleight of hand motions as ordinary motions like itching, adjusting glasses, etc. Also, implied assumptions are more believable than assertions by the performer. Researchers at Lund University in Sweden told individuals to pick out an attractive female from a set of photos, and then secretly switched the photos before asking why the chosen female was attractive. Most participants did not notice the switch and tried to justify their altered choice, thus displaying their "choice blindness." We are all guilty of defending our choices, when we are convinced they are the one we made (even if we didn't). The same principle is in play when the audience fails to notice the "man in a gorilla suit" while they are cognitively focused on some other activity. In an entertaining video available online, the magician and academic Richard Wiseman demonstrates a similar effect when he changes the back color of a playing card selected by his assistant. However, during the trick, several other items have also changed color, including the tablecloth, their shirts, and the background. Having been cued in to watch the cards, we miss these changes, suggesting that even though we may be looking at something directly, we may still not be paying any attention to it.

In pickpocketing, thieves use two hand motions to misdirect their mark's attention. Smooth motions activate the "pursuit" tracking system, which can draw gaze away from a theft, while erratic motions activate the "saccadic" system, which can suppress the mark's vision as the eyes lock onto new targets. Additionally, curved motions are harder to process and attract more attention than linear motion. "Illusory correlation" is the term for when a subject associates a cause and effect relationship between two sequential events (for example, the Misers Dream effect, expertly performed by Al Flosso or Teller). Thus, pickpockets, like magicians, are mostly exploiting the holes of our perception, instead of purely relying on the deftness of their fingers. Apollo Robbins, a stage pickpocket with a deep knowledge of the science of persuasion, demonstrates these effects deftly, and his marks are soon parted with all valuable possessions on their person. Robbins famously used his skills on the former US President Jimmy Carter's Secret Service detail in 2001, and relieved them of their badges, Carter's itinerary, a watch, as well as keys to the Presidential motorcade. Robbins ended up being approached by the Department of Defense to consult on the military applications of pickpocketing, behavioral influence, and con games. For a time, the Defense department was considering setting up a research-and-training facility at Yale University, and appointing Robbins as an adjunct professor there, but this initiative did not come into fruition. Fortunately, Robbins limits his demonstrations to the stage, and fastidiously returns all of his victim's possessions, even as they are left gasping in surprise. As author Adam Green, writes in a fascinating *New Yorker* profile on Robbins, he has fine-tuned these skills over the years, and has borrowed knowledge liberally from fields like aikido, the science of persuasion, and Latin ballroom dancing. The neuroscientist Susana Martinez-Conde, author of the book *Sleights of Mind*, formerly a researcher at the Laboratory of Visual Neuroscience in Arizona and now the director of the Laboratory of Integrative Neuroscience at the State University of New York, has closely studied how Robbins is able to achieve these startling effects. Magicians and conjurers uses the same body of knowledge, which they can also deploy on stage when needed. Through all these examples, it is clear that the art of magic is a strong and undeniable reminder of the weaknesses of human cognition.

In a paper that appeared in Nature Reviews–Neuroscience, an impressive range of magicians including Teller, John Thompson, Apollo Robbins, James Randi and Mac King teamed up with neuroscientists Stephen Macknik and Susana Martinez-Conde to come up with a taxonomy of conjuring effects, based on earlier work by Lamont and Wiseman. These are the first attempts in the scientific literature of trying to organize the principles by which magicians have operated over a long period of time. According to the authors, conjuring can take on a number of magical end effects, depending on the methods used. A brief description of these effects is provided below along with illustrative examples. Most professional magicians will use these in conjunction with verbal misdirection and usually use a combination or series of techniques to demonstrate the same effect, thus confusing the viewer.

1. Appearance: The first type of conjuring effect is "appearance" where "an object appears as if by magic." Appearance tricks employ three strategies: that "the object was already there but was concealed" (like hiding a coin in the hand before pretending to have it appear), "the object was secretly put into position" (like the "cups and balls" trick, where objects are inserted under the cups during the trick), and "the object is not there but seems to be" (like a psychic conjuring a spirit by secretly touching a spectator). There are many examples of this kind of effect, like the magician pulling a rabbit out of a hat, producing cards from thin air, or making an assistant appear from inside an empty box.

2. Vanishing: The second type of effect is "vanishing," where "an object disappears as if by magic." Vanishing tricks also employ three standard strategies. The possibilities are that

the object was never there at the start but the impression was given that it was, the object was secretly removed by a magician with the use a "gimmick," a secret device, to pull something into her sleeve, or the object never moved, but was concealed. An example of a vanishing effect is David Copperfield's vanishing of the Statue of Liberty, or Houdini's vanishing of an elephant. A vanishing is the reverse of the first effect, appearance or production.

3. Transposition: The third type of effect is "transposition," where an object appears to move from point A to point B. The four strategies for this effect are that the object seemed to be at A but already was at point B, the object is still at A but seems to be at B, the object was secretly moved from A to B, or a duplicate object was used. An example of this is Penn & Teller's Hanging Man trick, where Penn is apparently hanged but shows up safe in the audience. The Metamorphosis is another famous trick that uses a very fast form of this effect, and several variations of this are used by magicians nowadays.

4. Restoration: The fourth type of effect is "restoration," when an object is destroyed but then restored to its original condition. The strategies employed in this effect include: to either not really destroy the object, not really restore the destroyed object, or to use a duplicate mid trick. An example of this effect would be to saw an assistant in half (the object is never really destroyed).

5. Penetration: The fifth type of effect is "penetration," when objects seem to magically move through other objects (this effect is also sometimes referred to as "solid-through-solid". The main idea of penetration is to blend the strategies of restoration with those of transposition. An example is the Chinese Linked Rings trick, where "metal rings link and unlink magically." This effect can also be achieved by cleverly constructed props which shrink or expand under the control of the magician. Criss Angel demonstrates this effect when his body seems to penetrate a solid fence or a glass window.

6. Transformation: The sixth type of effect is "transformation," when an object changes its form. The main strategies for transformation are: to mix appearance of object A with vanishing of object B, or to secretly switch object A and B, or have A disguise as B or B disguise as A mid-trick. Examples of this would be the "Spellbound" trick, where a coin appears to turn into different coins by magic, changing colors on a silk handkerchief, or a gorilla in a cage changing into the magician's assistant.

7. Extraordinary Feats: The seventh effect is "extraordinary feats," which include mental and physical feats. The general strategy for this class of effects is to rely on obscure technical knowledge, like knowing that walking on coals does not result in burn injuries. Further examples include extraordinary abilities of calculation, like quickly multiplying large numbers, and invulnerability, like Penn & Teller's bullet-catching trick. Mentalism, if done well, can be a powerful form of magic performance, as it can fool people at a distance. This is very much unlike physical conjuring, where proximity to the performer can play an important role in the trick's ability to surprise or shock, and it is harder to discern the effects at a distance.

8. Telekinesis: The eighth effect is "telekinesis," which includes magical levitation or object animation. The main strategies for implementing telekinesis are: to have an external or internal force cause the action (like having a string pull something, or the use of magnetism), or to have the action not actually occur (as in the bent spoon trick). The two main examples of telekinesis are levitation and spoon bending.

9. Extrasensory Perception: The ninth and final effect is "extrasensory perception," like mind control, telepathy, and clairvoyance. The main strategies employed for this effect are to give the spectators the illusion of choice/free will by controlling their choices, fishing for information (either reading pre-written info or pumping info from the participant), and revealing proof that information revealed by the spectator was already known by the performer (maybe by hiding information in a "sealed" envelope that is opened

later). An example of this effect would be clairvoyance, which is acquiring information that is unknown to others through ESP. This is usually demonstrated when the magician successfully 'predicts' the outcome of some event based on their special knowledge.

Another effect that some categorize separately, is that of levitation. The basic idea there is to appear to defy gravity, and make something float in the air. This has included everything from floating a table (neatly demonstrated by the magician Losander) to floating an assistant (Robert-Houdin making his son Emile levitate). To successfully pull off these effects, magicians typically follow a handful of principles. First, "every action employed is a motion that has a purpose," meaning that actions that must be hidden should be explained away as trivial movements, like adjusting glasses when hiding something in the mouth, or touching one's hair while tucking in an object behind the ear. This means that the magician, during the many practice sessions that precede the actual performance, has to actively deconstruct every step of their routines, and pay careful attention to the sequencing and flow of specific actions. The second principle they need to heed carefully is the one dealing with "apparent repetition, priming, and 'closing all the doors'. Here, the magician's goal is to repeat an action or set of actions to either accustom a spectator to seeing the same sequence of steps, or to fool the spectator into thinking that a trick is performed the same way before changing the mechanism. The third principle is "never to do the same trick twice". The reason for this is straightforward. If a trick is repeated with the exact same method, the audience can easily figure it out. By introducing variations like repetition, unrelated gestures or actions, and multiple methods, magicians are able to successfully steer their audiences away from developing clear solutions or cracks to their tricks in real time. The use of these rules in combination with a thorough knowledge of the main categories of conjuring effects gives magicians the body of knowledge and the practical insights to fine tune their performance.

In a recent thesis published at Oxford University, Matthew Tompkins argues that magicians should be getting a lot more credit for their innovative breakthroughs. Their successful use of misdirection in particular has anticipated developments in scientific field of experimental psychology by hundreds of years; and in turn, the field of experimental psychology has benefited from focusing on the study of magic tricks and illusions. Despite the increased interest in magic as an area of scientific study, the approaches that have been suggested to date are very divergent, and there is no common agreement among scientists towards a common approach or body of knowledge. While one group has suggested a generalized psychology based theory of magic, another has focused primarily on the neuroscience of magic. Yet another group of scientists argue that focusing on a science of magic is a futile effort. Instead, the focus should be on limited and specific aspects of magic that can advance scientific understanding: there is no science of magic but just science itself. As this group led by the eminent magic scholar Peter Lamont neatly puts it using a magical phrase, the science of magic may just be an illusion, and that we should stop chasing after it. It remains to be seen whether science can successfully classify and explain all the intricacies of magic, or utilize the insights derived from analysis to better understand how the brain works. As of now, it seems like magicians have the edge over scientists in terms of their understanding of the basic principles employed and their ability to successfully use them in practice. They have earned this through thorough and systematic field testing over a long period of time, in full view of curious and observant audiences, including knowledgeable experts and peers.

Chapter 3: The Penn and Teller Effect: Modest Beginnings to the Pinnacle of Success

"I didn't learn fire-eating to conquer my fears. I learned fire-eating because I desperately wanted to be in show business."

—Penn Jillette

I always assumed I'd spend my life happily performing in artsy-fartsy little theaters.

—Teller

The Penn and Teller Effect

The Fédération Internationale des Sociétés Magiques (International Federation of Magic Societies), more commonly known as FISM, is a unique institution in the magic industry. It brings together more than 97 magic societies from around the globe, and represents approximately 70,000 magicians from 49 countries. FISM conducts one of the most prestigious magic gatherings in the world, the triennial "World Championships of Magic", the most recent iteration of which was held in South Korea in 2018. A lot of French is spoken and champagne is drunk, but that is not the primary purpose of this gathering. Magicians come here to demonstrate their newest magical creations, and to win the recognition of their peers. To win in any of the categories of this championship is to achieve the highest professional recognition in the magic community, and also speaks volumes about the sheer talent of the winners themselves. Competitions at this level are like the Olympics of magic, and to win the FISM Grand Prix award is considered the highest honor, and the winner joins a truly elite group. The participants have to come armed with the best ideas and the guts to perform in front of very knowledgeable peers who will be watching their every move. Besides the highest honors, the Grand Prix awards in Stage and Close-Up magic, prizes are awarded across several categories including manipulation, general magic, illusions, mentalism, comedy, micro-magic, card magic, parlor magic, and invention.

In 2015, an extremely talented and mysterious performer appeared for the first time on *Penn and Teller: Fool Us*. During his presentation, he did a set of card tricks that left the audience and Penn and Teller mesmerized and astounded by his skill and presentation. I am talking of course of Shin Lim. A prodigiously talented performer who had won the 2015 FISM World Championship award in Close-Up Card Magic at the competition held in Italy, Shin Lim is now considered the foremost exponent of this form of performance. Traditionally, magicians have relied on maintaining a steady patter to aid their demonstrations, i.e. a verbal routine in parallel with their visual manipulation and presentation. Visual tricks accompanied by a verbal commentary can greatly enhance the effect. However, Shin Lim is unique in that he relies on almost no commentary to complement his routines. Shin came up with his silent act after his experience on a 23-city tour of China. After seeing his performance at FISM in 2012, a tour organizer asked him if he could join this tour. Given his lack of fluency in Chinese, Lim had to drastically reconsider his act, which up to then relied on him talking to the audience. Lim worked on his routine to eliminate all speech during the act, and using only gestures in synchronization with the music, he created a new persona for himself. It is his signature style now, and he has used it in all his award-winning performances. His familiarity with music is a great help however, as it helps him set the mood and pace during his routines, and creates a unique dramatic effect that does not require any dialog. Lim is clearly a tenacious performer, and has had to overcome other obstacles, including suffering from carpal tunnel syndrome, and a serious injury to his thumb tendons which put him out of commission for a few months.

The video of Shin Lim's *Fool Us* performance that was uploaded on YouTube was one of the most viral videos ever, and has garnished over 53 million views. He went on to win *America's Got Talent* Season 13, in an extremely competitive field, and on a show that had only fielded mediocre magicians to date. He was of course invited back to Penn and Teller in Season 2, where he managed to fool them again. Jillette considers Shin Lim as being at the vanguard of a third-wave of magicians. His act contains elements of spectacle, along the lines of those popularized by David Copperfield and Doug Henning, but also includes a huge component of audience reactions or reactivity, a form perfected by David Blaine. Jillette expresses satisfaction that magic is returning in some ways to its roots, emphasizing skill and art over bravado and spectacle. As he put it in an interview, "I love that the Siegfried & Roy, David Copperfield, Doug Henning era is over. I love that the David Blaine and clone era is over. I love that there's this era of magic that is pure and honest and direct and sweet and beautiful." Lim's adherence to silence, his use of deliberate and purposeful gestures in perfect synchrony with the music, and the strategic use of special effects like smoke emanating from the table or from his mouth, add to the element of mystery in his routines. While the routines are carefully choreographed with nothing being left to chance, the audience is transported into a magical realm by the sheer visual spectacle. The most interesting part about Shin Lim's story is how he got interested in magic. Purely by accident, his elder brother showed him a YouTube clip that described a magic trick involving sleight of hand. Shin was completely hooked, and soon he was practicing up to eight hours a day, and learning voraciously through YouTube, as well as other sources. He could very well be the most important self-taught magician of the YouTube generation.

While you could argue that Shin Lim's raw talent and polished performance does not depend on a platform like Penn and Teller's show, there is no doubt that his appearance turbocharged his name recognition, fan following, and eventual commercial success. Other magicians who have appeared on the show have gone on to achieve similar results. In November of 2018, I had the opportunity to talk with Ryan Hayashi. A high-energy performer who fooled Penn and Teller with his version of a coin trick he calls the Ultimate Coin Matrix (which he performed with four coins and four playing cards), he told me something I did not expect to hear. After his performance on Penn and Teller, he said he has simply changed professions–he is now a magician. For many years, Ryan Hayashi has been a successful performer–but as the world's "most famous samurai entertainer". In this role, he has performed in 18 countries around the world in 8 different languages, and also appeared in several talent contests in Europe and Asia, among them, Germany's Got Talent, Britain's Got Talent, and Czechoslovakia's got Talent. In many of these appearances, Hayashi performed impressive feats, including cutting vegetables placed in people's mouths with a samurai sword while being blindfolded. Growing up idolizing Bruce Lee and David Copperfield, Hayashi discovered the parallels between martial arts and magic. Both have a long history and tradition, and also require dedication, practice, precision and a polished routine or flow. Hayashi believes that shows like *America's Got Talent* have traditionally not made enough effort to carefully scout or chase the best magicians. But that has changed a little since the success of Mat Franco. A card magician who was able to impress the judges with a variety of personalized close-up tricks, Franco won the contest and became the first magician to do so in its history. However, with the victory of Shin Lim on *America's Got Talent*, things have really changed, and it is clear that *Got Talent* finally gets magic, both as a crowd pleaser and an important component of the variety entertainment it offers. This, combined with the consistently high viewer ratings of *Fool Us*, seems to suggest that magic is finally back as part of the popular mainstream. The *Got Talent* franchise has been so successful that by 2014, there were spinoffs of the show in 58 countries. Another talent show scheduled to be released in 2019 attempts to overcome some of the criticisms of previous such competitions by broadening both the number of genres of performance, as well as the size, expertise and diversity of the judges' bench. On February 3rd, 2019, after the airing of the Super Bowl LIII game, CBS will be launching *The World's Best*. Hosted by James Corden, host of *The Late Late Show with James Corden*, this show attempts to provide another launching pad for performers of all stripes, magicians included, to showcase their skills. The celebrity judges will include Drew Barrymore, RuPaul Charles and Faith Hill. The show is designed so that the contestants will not only have to win over the judges, but also pass muster with what CBS calls "the wall of the world", a roster of fifty judges chosen across various fields of expertise.

Hayashi appeared on Penn and Teller *Fool Us* which aired on July 9th, 2018. He recalls how his appearance immediately began trending on Reddit and within the first four weeks had reached 5 million views on YouTube. His performance went viral very fast. He believes the overall presentation touched an emotional chord with the audience. Though it was his first time on American television, and his first time ever doing pure close up magic on TV; he did not come unprepared. In the past, he had had done 11 years of national prime time television, once in Brazil, twice in Japan, and the rest in Europe, in 12 different countries, in 6 different languages, and over 38 TV shows, so he brought a proper amount of experience onto the show. But all his prior appearances were to showcase his sword skills and not his magic. The reaction to his Penn and Teller appearance was so overwhelmingly positive that he has literally made the decision to hang up his swords (no pun intended) and take up magic as his calling. Though Hayashi is based in Germany, his travel plans soon looked like they would involve North America as he was getting booked for magic shows in traditional venues as well as for talks on the motivational speaker circuit. Following his appearance, Hayashi had to endure a grueling schedule which involved performing 31 back-to-back shows at the Magic Castle in Hollywood in Las Angeles in November, and moving on to Washington D.C. to do a motivational speaker's conference as a mindset speaker and success coach, and returning back to his base in Europe. The before and after effect here is truly game changing. Hayashi's variation on a classic routine, The Coin Matrix had been a hit. Combined with his smooth handling, and his ability to communicate highly effectively, by delivering "the most epic monologue in the history of magic," Hayashi not only wowed the audience, and fooled Penn and Teller, but also changed his career direction and future prospects. Today, Hayashi boasts over fifteen thousand subscribers on YouTube, whom he periodically entertains with clips from his talks and magic performances around the globe.

I like to think of this as the "Penn and Teller effect". For a lot of magicians, especially those who have not had national or international exposure, it is a forum where their five minutes on stage can literally change their career trajectory. It is in some ways immaterial if the magician fools Penn and Teller with their trick, but they definitely need to be entertaining and memorable. Penn has mentioned in interviews that the point of them trying to reveal the performing magician's methods is to show the audience that there are no camera tricks involved. Also, Penn and Teller understand the work put into a technique, unlike traditional reality judges who are not in the magic business. The idea behind the show is really to showcase talented magicians who would otherwise not get recognition. And Penn and Teller themselves are very supportive of magicians even if they were not fooled by their acts. Reports of their interactions backstage frequently mention them being very encouraging, offering tips and suggestions, and simply happy to see the new faces they have been successfully attracting to magic. Most importantly, all performers are completely confident of Penn and Teller's ability to judge their tricks, and accept their judgement without hesitation or conflict. This would not be the case where they question the competence or ability of the judges to gain insights on their acts. Though an appearance on *Fool Us* gives magicians between five and eight minutes to wrap up their performances, that time can literally change their lives, especially if they managed to fool Penn and Teller, but also if they were able to deliver a unique and memorable performance. A number of performers who have appeared on the show have seen their careers literally transformed by the experience. In the section below, I highlight a handful of such names, in addition to the ones already mentioned.

One of the more amusing appearances on Penn and Teller involved the Belgian magician, Jo De Rijck. In his act, Alyson Hannigan first established a "mental link" with Rijck's avian partner, a chicken named Curry. Alyson was then given a set of cards on which she had to write down things she would like to do on her "bucket list". However, only one of these choices was to be a real choice, and the others were things that sounded equally plausible but not what Alyson really wanted to do. These cards were then strung up. The chicken then walked back and forth and finally picked the card with Alyson's choice. After examining the card, and testing out some possible theories, Penn and Teller could not identify how the trick was done. They had been fooled by a chicken.

Following the show, Jo De Rijck was exploring a tour in the United States. This would increase his exposure from his traditional markets, Belgium and the Netherlands, where he does over five hundred shows a year. In addition, he also plans to do more shows in Germany and France, and is practicing both his German and French for that purpose. He is mum about whether he travels with the same chicken (Curry) or whether he has stand-ins. His own experience is that birds we don't give a second thought to and frequently end up on our dinner plates, are actually very intelligent. And as his performance showed, also very good stage partners.

Stuart MacDonald has been performing magic for all his life, and has been able to do so despite maintaining a full-time job as a training and development analyst at Whirlpool Corp. He took a lesson from his management background, and in particular, from the concepts of lean manufacturing and continuous improvement, which he learnt at his employer. On a whim, he decided to employ these concepts on his magic act, and soon he was making steady and measurable improvements to his repertoire. His signature act, where he fetches objects and eventually bags of money thanks to the multiplying powers of a mirror, was developed with help from Gene Anderson, a well-regarded magician himself, along with Tobin Ost, a Tony nominated production designer. The effect is almost like watching a piece of theater, and MacDonald wraps the viewer in easily into the story. For his performance on *Penn and Teller: Fool Us*, he firstly redesigned the mirror, which was the central piece of his performance. He took up the challenge of performing and recording his act one hundred times in the last thirty days before his appearance, with the goal of finding one improvement on each day (he managed to do it 92 times). By dedicating an extraordinary amount of effort for minor improvements, he was able to present a very polished production when his time came on the big stage.

The mainstream American public's reaction to top-level magic performers has undergone a radical shift. As Hayashi mentions, the general reputation, the respect, and love for magic is now higher than it was in the past. This cannot be ascribed solely to *Penn & Teller: Fool Us*, but after five seasons with good ratings, and showcasing more magic than the general public has ever seen before, the show has played its part. Before *Fool Us* hit the airwaves, Hayashi observes, the average Joe or Jane had not seen a lot of high quality magic. If fortunate, they might have seen them at larger corporate events, or on a guest spot on late night shows like Letterman, The Late Show, or Jimmy Kimmel. Other than that, the only opportunity would have been to tune in to the David Blaine Show more than 15 years ago, and watch David Blaine, or watch Criss Angel on his own show. In essence, the general public was not exposed to that much magic, both in terms of diversity or quality, especially in-person or in high quality digital video formats. This has now changed fundamentally; and the average viewer at home has now probably seen dozens of magicians in their living rooms, and that too with crystal clear reception. As far as the younger generation is concerned, all they need is to enter *Fool Us* on YouTube and within an hour they can watch more top quality magic than members of the previous generations saw in their entire lives. Clearly, there has been a definite and sharp increase in the amount of exposure, and shows like *Fool Us* and the *Got Talent* franchise can take some credit for it. Another reason for this change is that magic routines lend themselves very well to viral marketing and word-of-mouth, especially through social media. Most routines are around five minutes long on average, making them a perfect slice of entertainment for viewing and sharing on mobile devices, especially during short breaks. And most magicians have encouraged this phenomenon, as these short clips make for the ideal promotional tool, driving traffic to their own websites and online offerings, and audiences for in-person shows. They can also use their social media presence as vital promotional tools, and alert their fans to their live performances, publications, merchandise or media appearances.

Another performer who appeared on *Fool Us* in 2015, Kostya Kimlat, started in magic as a child. He spent twenty years performing mainly to corporate audiences (he brands himself as the 'business magician') before getting his first television appearance on the show. Kimlat was recommended to be on *Fool Us* by Johnny Thompson, one of the living legends of magic. Thompson is considered one of the few experts of magical craft, and consults with every popular magician in the business. At first Kostya was nervous about performing for Penn and Teller, so he read all of their published literature and watched all of their recordings. One concern was the selecting from the variety of tricks that Kimlat could perform, but another was the reality format of the show. Kimlat is no fan of traditional reality television, where he thinks artists compete and are judged by people who do not understand the work put into the art. However, *Fool Us* is not like a traditional show, because the magicians do not really compete with each other, they only try to fool Penn and Teller, who have no credibility problem unlike reality TV judges. For his performance, Kimlat decided to do an original piece that would showcase his mastery of close-up magic, and involve Penn and Teller themselves acting as participants and observers. Kimlat finally decided on a classical trick that he had done repeatedly, but with a relatively unknown twist. While practicing, Kimlat continued to evolve the technique. He finally relaxed when he concluded that his job was not to fool Penn and Teller, but to simply showcase his work to the best of his abilities. He pulled off the trick in spectacular fashion, and the reaction of Penn to being fooled is hilarious to watch.

After his appearance on the show, Kimlat moved to doing close-up magic with a lot more audience interaction, and immediately noticed that people were more excited to be around him and expected more of him because of his *Fool Us* appearance. Instead of keeping his performance quiet as a surprise, his clients started advertising his appearance to create a buzz. He was no longer an anonymous magician who was good, but a magician "who had fooled Penn and Teller". Kimlat mentions that while this change made his job easier, he also missed the challenge of overcoming a skeptical crowd. Although he is not a household name yet, he is glad that he waited so long to go on television, and he appreciates how small-scale acts made him a more focused and effortful performer.

Joshua Jay, a New York City based magician and author, has performed in over 100 countries, and he was awarded the top prize at the World Magic Seminar in 1998. Among his other achievements, he also holds a Guinness World Record for Most Selected Cards found from a shuffled deck in one minute. He found twenty-one cards in that time. In his appearance on Fool Us, he managed to fool Penn and Teller with a trick featuring a blank deck. He was surprised that he managed to fool them given their analytical bent, but was happy he did. After his appearance, Jay was contacted by a few companies who hired him for shows on the strength of that appearance. While he thinks that an appearance helps with credibility, not every magician can necessarily capitalize on it. He cites Piff (the Dragon) and Kostya Kimlat who have done a good job in building upon the appearance in concrete ways. In 2008, partnering with a close friend, Joshua founded Vanishing Inc., a manufacturer and distributor of props to magicians, as well as a retail magic outlet. Vanishing Inc. has grown to become one of the largest magic stores in the world, with warehouse and shipping operations in the US and Europe.

Another entertaining performer, Vinny Grosso, made the choice of performing his trick in his birthday suit on his first appearance (shielded by a small screen). His motto in magic is to be "Exposed and Fearless", which also happens to be the title of his book about successful performance artists. In his return appearance, he jokingly remarked that when people see him in public, they expect him to be naked, and are a bit disappointed that he is not. These anecdotes reveal the magical reach of Fool Us, and the ability of Penn and Teller to not just to become part of the cultural discourse in unexpected ways, but also key trend makers and influencers. The fact that many of these performances can be consumed in bite sized portions on YouTube and other online venues further adds to their appeal and impact.

The Early Days

Penn Jillette (b. 1955) and Raymond Teller (b. 1948), more famously known as Penn and Teller, have been performing for over forty years since they first met in 1975 at the Minnesota Renaissance Festival. At that time, Teller was teaching Latin at an Amherst,

Mass. prep school and Penn was washing dishes at the local Howard Johnson's. They were in fact introduced to each other by Weir Chrisemer, and the three of them started performing as a trio from the late seventies through the early eighties. Teller also performed at college parties, and found that he could exploit his quiet nature by dimming the lights and silently performing "disturbing" acts. And given that he maintained his silence, hecklers would have a tough time with someone who never spoke back. Prior to meeting Penn, Teller and his friend Weir Chrisemer had begun performing as The Othmar Schoeck Society for the Preservation of Weird and Disgusting Music. Once Penn joined the team, they called themselves "The Asparagus Valley Cultural Society" and played to audiences in Petaluma, California at the Phoenix Theater. Chrisemer was behind one of Penn and Teller's popular routines, Shadows, involving a rose. Teller appears on stage holding a gleaming carving knife, and standing in front of a rose in a vase. Projected behind him on a white screen is the image of the image of the same setup. He then proceeds to cut off the leaves and flower in the projected image. The real elements of the rose in the vase fall off at the same time, as if motivated by what is happening on screen. Though Penn does not make an appearance, the effect is simple but stunning, and Shadows went on to be one of the duo's most famous performances, and has been called one of the five iconic magic tricks of all time. This signature Teller routine later became the subject of a lawsuit when a Dutch magician Gerard Bakardy uploaded a video of another version of this trick on YouTube titled 'The Rose and Her Shadow', offering to sell his method for the sum of $3050. Teller filed a lawsuit against Bakardy alleging unfair competition and copyright infringement as he had rejected all settlement proposals. In a dramatic move, the federal court handed a victory to Teller, making it the first time the Copyright Act was amended since 1976, with the court ruling that a magic trick is eligible for protection, even if it was only presented as a dramatic work.

Specializing in illusions and a strong interaction with the audience, Penn does most of the talking, and Teller's typically maintains a studied silence, though engaging in mime and gestures as necessary. Despite the stark differences in their stage personas,

Penn being outspoken, gregarious, opinionated and brash, and Teller being silent, stoic, and slightly mysterious, both share a fondness for irreverence and zany humor, and love to clue the audience in even as they are misdirected or tricked. Penn and Teller became a successful magic act by incorporating popular skills like juggling and escapology into a contemporary and complex theatrical performance. Their acts derive from their desire to be different, and their roots as sideshow admirers, as they often satirize their contemporaries, simplify their acts, and deconstruct their own tricks. In other words, even while performing, they also take the point of view of the audience, and often poke fun at themselves, often leading to unexpected sources of humor and entertainment. During their childhoods, they were primarily focused on variety skills, and learned simple tricks early on.

Growing up with the new broadcast medium of the time, television, Teller saw a need for realism, and appreciated the darker elements and the genuine emotion of good acting. Penn, on the other hand, was heavily influenced by the lack of audience interaction on television (which is why he makes extreme efforts to interact), and also enjoyed dark humor and punchline driven stories like the Twilight Zone. Penn went to clown school (yes, there is such a thing) and went on to focus on juggling. As Penn's juggling abilities improved, he became a hitchhiker and made money through his juggling act and literally passing the hat to earn money. He soon found he was getting good at drawing a crowd, and his menu of juggling items expanded to include balls and knives, in addition to doing some of the routines blindfolded. He would perform his juggling act at the Headhouse Square in Philadelphia, and could draw a big crowd thanks to his height, loud voice and imposing personality. While juggling, he would also volubly talk about what he was doing, almost as if he was disassociated from the performance. The audience clearly loved this and Penn was soon raking in up to six hundred dollars for a twelve -minute act. This was big money in the seventies. When Penn went to his accountant and described how much money he was making, the accountant remarked that he would get charged for selling drugs. Teller thinks that the twelve-minute act that Penn did in those days was one of the best performances he has ever done. Penn has continued his juggling act until recently, and on a recent Fool Us episode, as he juggled three broken bottles, he held forth his trademark conversation with the audience without missing a beat despite the obvious concern written all Alyson Hannigan's face.

Penn and Teller started performing together as a duo in 1981. Teller developed his characteristic persona as the quiet and introspective counter to Penn. During shows with Chrisemer, they experimented with unorthodox techniques and audience participation. This is when they discovered parody as an effective tool to entertain their audiences. For example, during Penn's juggling act, "Starter Kit," he deconstructs the act and explains all its aspects in parody while still performing. Teller does a parody of traditional magic shows called the "Duck Trick." These were the prototypes for their later acts. The trio eventually broke up and the dominant (and contrasting) personalities of Penn and Teller soon established themselves as the creative team. For a brief period, they also branched into a dark theatre format with Mrs. Lawnsbury's Séance of Horror. After this, they participated in a cross-country series of street shows, while developing new material and redesigning their theatrical shows, and finally transitioned to off-Broadway engagements in New York City at the Westside Arts Theatre.

A modest building constructed in 1890 as Second German Baptist Church, the Westside Theatre is located in the Hell's Kitchen neighborhood of Manhattan. This building proved to be the diminutive launching pad for their national and eventually global success. In a promising review, Frank Rich of the New York Times called their show "one of the season's most original infusions of fun". Realizing that their performances would be better suited to theatre performances than smaller venues, Penn and Teller decided to start writing a longer show and working in Los Angeles. They first adjusted to using lighting, which was expected in a professional theatre, relegating their techniques of blackouts to reflect the mood in their darker acts. They developed a difference between fantasy and reality, and established creative violence as a theme in their acts. They also focused on demystification and deconstruction, expanding it to general theme of trick-busting, which they used to dramatic instructional effect. Teller's fascination with spirit media moved the demystification trend into that of debunking psychics. As their theater presence grew, they hired Art Woolf, John Lee Beatty, and Dennis Parichy as directors and designers. They maintained the sideshow style atmosphere while adopting business suits to build a contradictory look. Their tricks used naked magic, by deliberately not trying to hide what is being done, but instead focusing on the tension, dark overtones, and storytelling to entertain. They also satirized traditional magic acts, which they believed to be unoriginal or weak. Several satires and tricks, including Teller's needle trick, comprised the first act, while the second acts were typically much darker and less down-to-earth.

After this phase, when P&T moved to Broadway, they cut out anything that was not explicitly developed for their theater show, like carnival tricks, and focused on just magic and their characters. After Broadway, they expanded into different forms of media, including video and television, making appearances on TV shows and interviews. They placed a great deal of emphasis on writing their shows to fit their medium, meaning the size and location of their venues. They were also pioneers in interacting with their audience during intermission and after the show. They have claimed that their most important belief is not to insult or belittle their audience, which is reflected in their explanation and interaction styles. This also marked a significant change from how past magicians used to approach the audience: the expectation previously was that the magician was the one on the mighty pedestal, to be admired and celebrated. However, Penn and Teller demolished this notion by portraying themselves on the same level as the audience, through their interactions, by looking at things from the audience point of view, and their ability to laugh at themselves. As one scribe put it, their "whose sleight of hand is never intended to sleight the audience of intelligence". This was a very different approach than the one taken by David Copperfield, for instance, who cuts a more iconic figure, with the audience being the clear subordinate to his prowess. This emphasis on audience interaction and reaction has been carried on to a different level by magicians like David Blaine and Dynamo, where it is an integral part of their entire routine.

Expanding the Audience:
Going Public and Forays in Television

In 1985, the duo debuted a TV special on PBS, *Penn and Teller Go Public*, and went on to perform on a successful off-Broadway run. The show itself was well received, and won two Emmys. They soon moved to Broadway, where their success with the show continued. In the 90s, they continued their touring and crisscrossed the country several times. They also presented the updated "Sorcerer's Apprentice" segment in Disney's Fantasia 2000. With continued touring, and nationwide recognition and coverage, including on the late-night talk circuit with Letterman and Leno, SNL, and as guests on The Simpsons, and other cameos on shows like Babylon 5, Sabrina the Teenage Witch and The West Wing.

Penn and Teller soon expanded their abiding interest in TV. The format fit their style very well: while the longer specials and projects gave them time to demonstrate their interests and skills, the shorter appearances served as valuable promotional opportunities and means to connect to the audience. Among their may specials were Sin City Spectacular, Don't Try This at Home, Off the Deep End, and the Magic and Mystery Tour. The Penn & Teller's Magic and Mystery Tour was more in the format of a documentary, where they focused on street magic overseas. Despite the grainy video quality of the archives (by today's standards), you can still see their enthusiasm and wide-eyed wonder at discovering obscure and famous tricks the world over.

While Teller maintains his usual silent persona, except during an episode set in Egypt, Penn clearly enjoys every moment and one can see that he is totally comfortable interacting with street performers everywhere. Among the countries visited were China (where Penn juggled some broken bottles to impress a Chinese juggler), India (where they created an illusory Indian Rope Trick), and Egypt (featuring the Gali-Gali men). In 1994, they appeared in a TV show titled *The Unpleasant World of Penn and Teller*, in the UK. The thrust of this show was to clearly combine magic with comedy, in a bit to reclaim magic from the light entertainment fare that was popular on British TV at the time. While the revelation of some tricks on *Unpleasant World* caused consternation among the members of the Magic Circle, the show went over very well with the new younger demographic of Channel 4. This audience clearly enjoyed the type of participation and interaction that Penn and Teller fostered, and a format the audience were already used to through other shows in the comedy and game show genres.

Penn & Teller went on to present a show on the Showtime TV network entitled *Penn and Teller: BS*, in which they turned a skeptical eye on a number of topics. Some of the topics included the paranormal, conspiracy theories, and religion. The two men's quirky, broadly libertarian political and social views were frequently in evidence, with segments dealing with subjects ranging from the war on drugs to gun control. They have also authored several books on the subject of magic and caused some controversy within their profession by presenting a series of shows explaining how specific tricks were done. However, these were specially created for the programs, and did not reveal how other magicians perform their illusions. In a TV performance where they "showed" the audience how to do the cups and balls trick, using transparent cups, they actually showed a deft variation of the trick and its beauty, but did not really reveal anything about the trick. However, they faced a lot of backlash for doing this, especially from fellow magicians. We will discuss this more in a further chapter.

The four key sets of players in the magic industry, i.e. inventors, designers, builders, and performers together constitute an ecosystem where ideas and the economic benefits derived from them are constantly in circulation. This suggests that trust is a critical component that makes this ecosystem successful, as the various stakeholders are constantly engaged in exchanging 'secret' knowledge. This brings us to an interesting observation by scholars who study intellectual property. Despite this trade in secrets, magic is one of the fields where intellectual property law offers almost no protection to these innovators. You might expect that innovation itself would not thrive under such a loose regime, but interestingly, magic seems to be a very fertile ground for innovation. IP scholars have seen similar patterns in other industries as well. In the field of designer fashion, for example, it has been argued that top designers have no qualms about their designs being copied and moving down the value chain. It not only gives them greater clout as the original trendsetters, but also acts as a form of planned obsolescence. As a result, they can stay on top of the game by innovating at the top end of the market, while their previous designs slowly trickle down. In the case of magic, however, the norms are slightly different. Although there is protection of intellectual property within the community through informal processes and sanctions, there is no real need for intellectual property law itself. This is also referred to as the concept of 'negative spaces' in intellectual property law, since the conventional wisdom might have you believe that a legal framework supports and creates incentives for new ideas, and protection of existing ideas.

The International Brotherhood of Magicians and the Society of Magicians both follow a strict internal code of ethics. Unless explicitly permitted, members of these organizations are forbidden to reveal 'the modus operandi of magic effects or principles to the lay public'. Typically, exceptions can be granted when 'the intent is clearly to teach, so that the recipient may learn how to make and/or perform the effect or effects, rather than simply to satisfy curiosity'. Thus, under this clause, magician is more likely to reveal a trick to a student or dedicated apprentice rather than a curious spectator. Another exception is 'where the method of an effect is integral to the plot, as in a detective novel or play'. When magicians are called in as consultants in dramatic theater or film productions, they can get an exception, as some of the effects may require the construction or fabrication of complex props requiring the knowledge to be shared. Another exception is 'where the method is important to the history of the performer or inventor or the evolution of the effect under discussion, as in a magic history or biography', again a likely possibility in an academic setting or educational context. The final possible exception is 'where an effect is performed and then the simple method is revealed as a gag or stunt'. There could be other situations where a member maybe granted a privilege, but only on the determination that 'the Art of Magic is not injured thereby'. By establishing this set of shared expectations, as well as a series of custom exceptions, these societies try to balance the need for confidentiality and secrecy, with the more practical concerns of sharing and information exchange that magicians may face in practice.

In addition, it turns out that the magic community has developed its own set of norms for ensuring that inventors of new and prominent tricks get credit for their efforts. Not only that, even if the original effort is improved on in a subsequent iteration, the original inventor is always acknowledged and credited. The second set of norms deals with ideas that have already been created. The common agreement here is that if a secret method has not been widely shared, published, or sold, nobody else can use it; and if indeed has been widely shared, it may be used freely. Further, if a dramatic presentation has been widely shared, it may be used, but using it will be considered bad form, and if a trick was originally published or shared but has not been used for a long time, the person who re-discovers it can be considered the inventor. The final norm is the most important: a magician can never expose a trick to a non-magician. This last point is the one on which fellow magicians have cried foul, but the trend online is to reveal much more than what Penn and Teller have ever done. When Fox TV aired a special titled 'Breaking the Magician's Code: Magic's Greatest Secrets Revealed' in the Fall of 1997, the reaction from magicians was swift. Lawsuits were soon flying, thanks to the magician's contention that Fox was destroying their livelihoods by revealing trade secrets. The show revealed the inner workings of more than twenty-five illusions, in defiance of the outrage among magicians. The tricks were performed by the "Masked Magician" named Valentino. By analyzing the style of the performances, magicians quickly deduced that Valentino was none other than the performer Leonard Montano. Prior to the final special, Valentino himself revealed his true identity. In one of their lawsuits, magicians argued that revealing the illusions in this fashion was a violation of the Uniform Trade Secrets Act, since the owners of the "trade secret" derive economic benefit from keeping it secret. However, this ventured into a gray area as there was never a determination if any of the magic acts revealed on the show were actual trade secrets as defined by the law. Even in 1997-1998, at the time of airing of the show, most of the solutions to the inner workings of the tricks being exposed could be found in written work freely available for purchase, and also online during the early days of the Internet. Valentino later mentioned that he signed up under the agreement that he would only reveal the workings of "older" illusions, with the intention of motivating kids to take up magic. However, this view was derided by professional magicians who had invested time and money in creating special effects which helped them earn a living. We will discuss this issue further when we come to the case of complicated magic tricks and their solutions that proliferate on YouTube today, or avenues like Penguin Magic where one can simply purchase them outright, no questions asked. The key issue is whether such trends point to a demise in the future of magic, or whether they will perhaps end up opening up new frontiers by spurring more innovation.

Penn and Teller have continued to perform live most nights with the longest ever running show in Las Vegas at the Rio Hotel. The show also holds the distinction of being the longest running show at a hotel! On a recent family trip to Las Vegas, after checking in at the Bellagio, I discovered that my living room had a prime view on to the Rio Hotel in the distance. Boldly emblazoned on the facade of the building was a giant facade of Penn and Teller, acting as a solitary beacon in the desert to all fans and fellow performers, night and day (I took this as a sign that there was a book to be written!). Jillette has an interesting observation about audiences in Vegas. Unlike places like London or Chicago or New York, where fans book their tickets months in advance, and eagerly await the performances, he believes that Vegas audiences typically decide on attending the show very impulsively, frequently on the same day of the performance. His intuition is borne out by the numbers from actual survey data from the Las Vegas Convention and Visitors Authority. Jillette does however prefer performing to an understated audience with somewhat lower expectations, as he can then try hard to prove they made the right decision, rather than one that came in with extremely high expectations. In addition to jointly performing with Teller, Penn has also worked alone on a small number of projects. He presented NBC's Identity game show from 2006 onward. He also hosted a talk show on FM radio for just over a year beginning in early 2006. The duo was reunited on screen for the Discovery Channel's Tell a Lie series. They were included on the Hollywood Walk of Fame in 2013, with their star being close to Harry Houdini's.

Becoming a Recognized National Brand

As their careers took off, Penn and Teller's distinct traits and personalities took on even more importance as they became more recognizable. In many of their routines, Teller usually is the victim of Penn's tricks. In others, he is presented as the "wise one", while Penn is the talkative and rambling hack of a magician. In a memorable take in a later Fool Us episode (the one with Kostya Kimlat, mentioned earlier), Penn refers to himself as the "big, dumb guy", who can be easily fooled, but claims that it is really hard to fool Teller. They both stick to a dress code of business suits to preserve their modernity and present a clean-cut look, unlike other magicians whose wardrobe plays a more critical role in their presentation. Both men have stated that they drink no alcohol and also steer clear of caffeine and other drugs. In private, the two members of Penn and Teller have relatively little to do with each other, as magic is their only real shared interest. Despite being close friends and business partners, they live different social lives. Even though they live close to each other, they get a lot of their communication and teamwork done through email. Penn famously used to live in a large house outfitted with magic memorabilia and tech toys, named "The Slammer". All visitors to his residence would get their pictures taken (mugshots with a police lineup background), which would then be streamed on multiple television screens and computer monitors throughout the house. Though Penn joked that he wanted to shoot a horror movie at the home and have it destroyed in a final chaotic scene, he recently sold the home for $1.88 million. Teller's also likes to keep a house full of magic books and artefacts, complete with a secret passage hidden behind the bookshelves.

In an erudite analysis examining Penn and Teller's distinct performances, the academics Elizabeth Miller and Peter Zompetti convincingly argue that their acts can be classified as postmodern "anti-magic." What do they mean by this? For one thing, Penn and Teller have built a brand on satirizing conventional magic acts, and actively deconstructing them on stage. In their typical stage performances, they are particularly adept at switching between the two modes of ironic humor and macabre and dramatic horror. Some of their tricks in the latter genre have suggestive names like Bloody Hat Pin, Rodent Roulette and Hand Stab, and are intended to revolt and delight the audience at the same time with their unconventional approach. They also take inspiration from street magic practiced in other parts of the world, where blood and gore contribute to the morbid fascination of the gathering crowd, and every escalation by the magician is met with gasps of shock and disgust, but the crowd finds itself unable to avert their collective gaze. Add to this Penn's loud commentary, and their contrasting personalities, and the fun and zany characteristic of their performance is further amplified. Further, the duo aims to teach their audience to be skeptical of everything, especially magic, and consequently they have been instrumental in creating educated and more sophisticated audiences. The magic community seemingly adheres to two high-level rules intended to preserve the secrecy of their tricks. First, a magician should never tell the audience what the effect will be, and second, a magician should never repeat an act. These rules are frequently broken, but the magic community survives because the performance of a trick is more important than the technical details associated with it, and no two performers are perfectly alike. Also, repetition is frequently used in close-up magic: both repetition of effect (using different methods), and repetition of method, in the same trick. It all depends on the context, setting, and timing, and the sophistication of the audience. If the magicians feel they can get away with these moves without being discovered, they will choose to take the chance.

The goal of magic is to instill wonder in the audience rather than forward the act as an impossibility come to life. In secular magic, nobody (or at least the vast majority) ever believes in the occult or the supernatural. Also, challenging the audience to explain a magic trick will often turn them away, because it makes the show a competition, and performing oversimplified tricks also has the effect of insulting the audience's intelligence. To prevent this, magicians can use humor, specifically humorous incompetence. Humor can win audience support, and also prevent dark tones or ideas from overwhelming the audience. More importantly, humor plays a very important role in freezing the attention of the audience, allowing the performer to successfully use the time towards the next conjuring objective without the audience ever noticing.

Penn and Teller were inspired by Houdini to incorporate magic debunking into their routine. In the "Looks Simple" routine, Penn narrates Teller's silent cigarette trick and reveals how the trick works, while Teller introduces "wordless deception," lying through gesture. This act is a good example of the duo's personality dichotomy, as Teller silently performs while Penn comments. In their cup and balls act, they break the above two rules of magic by repeating the trick and using clear cups. They say that their version does not insult the intelligence of the audience. Showing the audience their process also helps divert audience attention by creating a false sense of inclusion, which lets them set up a larger ruse and remain undetected. They often incorporate irony into acts by playing on common tropes to both entertain and educate their audience. In their "shredding a rabbit" act, they satirize traditional tricks like card guessing and pulling rabbits out of hats by putting both the deck and the rabbit through a shredder. In the drowning trick, Teller "drowns" in a tank while waiting for Penn to finish a magic trick. Throughout this trick, Teller has the key to his own tank, but refuses to give it up unless Penn can finish the trick. These two tricks blend magic and dark humor for satirical effect. Penn and Teller often treat death with whimsy, because they disagree with overhyping the danger of magic. Through their comedy and nonchalant acting, they convey that the "gore" on stage is not serious. Their wry take on this is that they deconstruct the trick in great detail in order to shame other magicians into innovating on dead tricks.

Penn and Teller also break the rules by revealing how their "Blast Off" trick works by using clear props, and in their "sawing a woman in half" trick, they explain how conventional magicians do it, then they create a double illusion where they appear to accidentally mutilate their subject during the explanation. Both these examples utilize humor to full effect, and the latter example utilizes two levels of illusion, which they go on to explain after the act. The idea behind these explanations is to divert the audience's attention away from the mystical or supernatural and bring it down to earth with a thud. In some ways, they have now added a fourth stage to "pledge, turn, and prestige," which is the explanation that the audience resolution and satisfaction at the end. Penn and Teller instinctively know that not giving a resolution or closure can lead to audience dissatisfaction. Given their disposition to reveal the inner workings of tricks, or simply show them out in the open, they have attracted a lot of negative criticism. However, they strongly believe that they are not infringing on any proprietary magic, and want to shift the magic paradigm. Parodying magic in this way allows them to revive the art of magic, while simultaneously being "anti-magicians" and "magicians."

In their long-running show at the Rio in Las Vegas, Penn and Teller keep changing the elements of the show with every iteration, in order to keep it fresh and surprising. Many of their audience members are repeat visitors; and though they expect novelty and like surprises, they also expect to see some 'old standards'. Hence, there are some routines which are featured without fail, as audiences expect to see them. Two examples that Teller cites are the Shadows illusion that he has been performing for years, and is now considered his signature piece; as well as the duo's double bullet catch, which they have performed for over two decades. Jillette believes that this act is one of their crowd favorites and also fools the most people. One of the highlights of their performances is the fact that audience members can meet with them after the show, where they talk and pose with them for pictures in the hotel lobby, and stay on till every single audience member leaves satisfied. Penn and Teller have been doing this for over four decades and believe that it brings them closer to their audience. And they don't charge a dime for doing so either. This is different from the approach taken by other stars, where they view such "meet-and-greet" and "photo-op" sessions as additional ways to generate revenues, and occasions to be monetized. For example, David Copperfield charges over $100 for a meet-and-greet, whereas Olivia Newton-John, who performs at the Flamingo Hotel in Las Vegas, charges as much as $170 for a photo-op backstage.

Chapter 4:
The *BS* Years to *Fool Us*

The purpose of art is to collide the intellectual and visceral together at the highest speed possible.

—Penn Jillette

"You get into magic in order to be fooled. And when we were young and starting out, of course nearly every act fooled us. but it's like with magic, you're always searching the first high."

—Penn Jillette

BS: The Show Concept

First released in early 2003, this show, *Penn and Teller BS*, was predicated on Penn and Teller's ability to debunk popular fads and myths, with a particular emphasis on busting pseudoscientific or paranormal beliefs. The show had a very successful run on Showtime for the next seven years, and in the process garnered 11 Emmy nominations, while also becoming the longest running show on that network. Interestingly, the choice of the word 'bullshit' to describe the purveyors of aforementioned fads and scams was considered a safe choice. Calling them liars, quacks or scammers would have quickly opened up the possibility of lawsuits. As Penn mentions in his trademark style on the show, "So forgive all the 'bullshit language', but we're trying to talk about the truth without spending the rest of our lives in court." The show also included appearances by well-known skeptics like James Randi. A broad variety of topics was covered across the various episodes: some standouts include the influence of cults, alternative medicine, fad diets, Feng Shui, conspiracy theories, the paranormal, and creationism. Critics of the show have claimed that the discussions occasionally branch out into pseudo-skepticism and denialism, but there can be no denying that the show explored a wide variety of controversial topics.

Paranormal beliefs are phenomena that are defined as falling outside or not understood by current scientific knowledge. Psychologists have even constructed research instruments to try and measure the degree of belief in the paranormal. The PBS (Paranormal Belief Scale) is one such measure, where respondents are asked about things like their belief in the existence of witchcraft or mind-reading, for example. A revised scale introduced in 2004 tries to measure such beliefs along seven dimensions. These dimensions include: traditional religious belief, psi, witchcraft, superstition, spiritualism, extraordinary life forms, and precognition. A typical episode of *Penn and Teller: BS* would involve interviews with the proponents of various paranormal theories and beliefs and frequently trying to catch them in self-contradictory loops. One intriguing episode investigates the belief among several groups about alien technology and its links to Area 51. Located in a remote part of Nevada, Area 51 is a remote US Air Force detachment affiliated with the Edwards Air Force Base. Its remoteness and secrecy have given rise to a number of unverified conspiracy theories. These include the theory that the base is a primary site for the reverse engineering of captured alien aircraft, to it being a secure facility for the confinement of aliens themselves, be they dead or alive. In the episode, Penn and Teller make the case that these theorists are being very selective in the type of evidence they collect, and are predisposed to believing this evidence gathered through non-scientific methods. It could be that they are members of a community who share a passion for their belief in extraterrestrial life, and their 'studies' are essentially a hobby of sorts. Soon, these creative theories soon verge into the fantastical, and the use of selective evidence brings them into the realm of the plausible.

In some episodes, the focus is on more mundane topics, and Penn and Teller also carried out their own little pranks and experiments in both to entertain and educate. A popular episode "Bottled Water", which happens to be one of my favorites, has the magicians conducting a 'taste test' of various bottled waters, purportedly from exotic locations, with customers at a fancy restaurant. These volunteer testers dutifully discern subtle differences across the waters presented to them, thus establishing their sophistication and good taste. Soon, the secret is revealed. Penn and Teller have been filling all the bottles in the backyard with a garden hose and free municipal water! The only change was the presentation: different bottles, and different BS to describe each of their taste profiles. This is also their version of satirical social commentary on the state of the consumer economy.

One episode in this series for which Penn and Teller received a lot of flak is the one examining the effect of secondhand smoke. In the episode, they took the view that bans on smoking are an infringement of personal freedom, and presented anecdotal evidence from various people that they had not been impacted by second-hand smoke either. Of course, several scientific studies have shown that both smoking and second-hand smoking are significantly damaging, but these studies have been refuted by the tobacco industry. In fact, the tobacco industry even took legal action against such reports in the early nineties. However, several studies after that have continued to show the deleterious effects of smoking and exposure to secondhand smoke. In all fairness to Penn and Teller, they admitted later that they were most likely wrong about their inferences at the time of filming the show. Though this retraction was not too convincing given their disparagement of the scientific studies on the episode itself, the DVD release of the show carried a correction of their position. One wonders if the original objective of the claim was simply to be a bit controversial.

In another entertaining episode, the focus was on debunking the practice of Feng Shui. Three practitioners were separately allowed to arrange the same room according to the principles of Feng Shui, which is claimed as being "scientific". Turns out that each arrangement was not only completely different, the practitioners could not come up with a concrete definition of what the energies were which they were realigning through their exercise. One practitioner claimed that the "energies of chi are playing a cosmic game of musical chairs". Penn and Teller clearly enjoyed the absurdity of the situation and let the action speak for itself. They later profiled a beauty parlor which offers haircuts based on Feng Shui principles for the steep sum of a hundred and fifty dollars. Turns out it was not any more remarkable than a haircut costing sixteen dollars. Fans consider this to be one of the classic episodes which neatly encapsulates the initial premise of the show. It also brings to light the dubious practices used by vendors of pseudo-scientific theories, in areas where there is little to no empirical verification.

One aspect of the show that cannot be argued against is that Penn and Teller gave the widest possible platform to a diverse and eclectic group of people. The more wacky and controversial their positions, the better, for the sake of entertainment and the potential impact of the debunking. Among the (in)famous and questionable people featured on the show were folks like Roger Lear (a surgeon specializing in extracting alien implants), Bruce Breach (an eccentric doomsday prepper), Russell Targ (explaining his theories on remote viewing), and Joe Arpaio (who claims that legalized drugs would lead to doctors operating on patients while under the influence of the drugs themselves). Many of them went on to achieve their own version of fame, and in many cases, notoriety.

The Debunkers and the Debunked

There has been a long association between magicians and the art of debunking or exposing myths, superstitions and the paranormal. The term 'debunk' traces its origin to the novel Bunk, published in 1923 by American journalist William Woodward. As per Woodward, debunk could "take the bunk (or the nonsense) out of things". The term "debunkery" is not just restricted to debating scientific arguments. It could mean attempts to discredit any opposing point of view, including that of a rival or political opponent. The debunker thus also emerges as a passionate advocate for the public interest, while exposing scams, hacks and charlatans. One of the earliest known debunkers was Harry Houdini, who took it upon himself to expose frauds who claimed supernatural powers. Another early debunker was the English magician John Nevil Maskelyne, who first exposed the Davenport brothers and their spirit cabinet illusion in 1865. In order to expose the fraudulent spiritualists, Maskelyne, along with his cabinet maker friend George Cooke, built a bigger replica of the Davenport cabinet. They then staged the same illusion to audiences, even adding their own bit of comedy by having one of the performers wear a gorilla suit. A talented performer who is credited with inventing levitation, he was also the inventor of many devices including the 'pay toilet', and a co-inventor of Psycho, an automaton that played whist, a popular card game. He was the founder of the Occult Committee, a group founded with the aim of investigating claims to supernatural power and exposing fraud.

Debunking has evolved into an art form, as its practitioners must be very careful in how they apply their skills. Despite the name recognition and credibility of many debunkers, their efforts can often backfire. There are several reasons for this. In their zeal to debunk something, they may end up accidentally reinforcing the very beliefs they are trying to correct. This is also referred to as belief perseverance. There have been studies prescribing the best approach to debunking, and these involve simplicity, short messages, building up the subject's confidence and ego, and not trying to describe misconceptions or threatening the subject's worldviews. The believers generally tend to hold on strongly to their worldviews, and would rather be right in their convictions rather than believing facts. As one researcher describes this, in the absence of a better explanation, people choose to continue believing in the wrong explanation.

One such figure who established this genre firmly in the cultural landscape of the seventies was a close friend of Penn and Teller, the skeptic James Randi. A former practitioner of magic and escape acts, Randi retired from the profession to take up his new calling as a scientific skeptic and investigator (he dislikes the term debunker). A repeat guest on the Tonight Show with Johnny Carson, he exposed faith healers, con men and other purveyors of the paranormal and supernatural. His most famous target was the Israeli performer Uri Geller, who claimed that he could bend spoons using genuine psychic abilities, or telekinesis. In an appearance on the Johnny Carson show, the Israeli magician was famously humiliated when his magical powers did not seem to work. James Randi, collaborating ahead of time with the staff on The Tonight Show, had set them up to strictly observe and control all the props used during the performance, and ensure that Geller did not have access to them or switch them ahead of his appearance. Penn and Teller made an appearance in a biographical movie about James Randi, *An Honest Liar*, which was released in 2014.

Another classic exposure by Randi involved Peter Popoff, a faith healer who would seemingly know detailed personal information of audience members in his church gatherings. By establishing his credibility first by reciting arcane information like their addresses, afflictions, and names of family members, he would then "cure" them of their maladies. After a detailed investigation, Randi soon came across the source of these magical abilities. It turned out that Popoff was being fed this information over the air through a concealed earpiece. At the other end was his wife, transmitting this information that had been gleaned from the prayer cards that all of the churchgoers had filled out. While this might seem ordinary in retrospect, watching a video of the "faith healing" performance shows us how powerful the effect can be to a gullible audience who are putting their faith and hopes in their object of salvation. Penn Jillette has commented how much he is irritated by folks claiming to talk to the dead, not because they are making money by preying on the grief stricken, but rather because they cavalierly desecrate the family bonds and memories through their greed.

An initiative that Randi established, the James Randi Educational Foundation, famously sponsored the One Million Dollar Paranormal Challenge. This challenge offered a grand prize of one million dollars to any eligible applicants who could "demonstrate evidence of any paranormal, supernatural, or occult power or event under test conditions agreed to by both parties". After Randi's retirement, this challenge was terminated in 2015. More than one thousand people tried their hand at winning the prize, but none succeeded. In a wry comment, Randi observes that hardly any of the unsuccessful applicants give serious thought to the possibility that their failure to win the prize may be due to the fact that they simply do not possess the power they believe they do. Rather, they are more inclined to criticize the test conditions, or extraneous factors completely out of the scope of the experiment. Like Randi, Penn and Teller take a special delight in debunking theories and beliefs that do not hold up to the experimental test. Besides Houdini, James Randi, and Penn and Teller, other famous skeptics have included Stanton Friedman, Martin Gardner, Carl Sagan, Isaac Asimov, Richard Dawkins and Michael Shermer. Other magicians known for their skepticism include Ricky Jay, Christopher Milbourne, Steve Cuno, Criss Angel, and more recently, Derren Brown.

When the magician Jim Callahan suggested that one of his tricks on the TV show *Phenomenon* was aided by a spirit guide, Criss Angel offered $1,000,000 from his personal funds to Uri Geller and Jim Callahan if they could psychically determine the contents of an envelope in his hand. In an appearance on Larry King, Angel emphasized, "No one has the ability, that I'm aware of, to do anything supernatural, psychic, talk to the dead. And that was what I said I was going to do with *Phenomenon*. If somebody goes on that show and claims to have supernatural psychic ability, I'm going to bust them live and on television." Criss Angel has spoken out against the practice of mediumship, and has gone on to say that he would go out of his way to expose them, even if they were members of his own family. He is of the opinion that people claiming to communicate with the dead should be exposed as they prey on innocent and vulnerable victims. Similarly, Derren Brown is particularly interested in going after those who pose as faith healers and mediums. Though known as Britain's most famous mind-reader, he makes it clear to his audience that he primarily uses suggestion, psychology, misdirection, and showmanship to achieve his effects, and nothing more. In his live stage shows, like *Svengali*, and through his TV show, *Derren Brown: The Experiments*, Brown frequently demonstrates how the public can be misled by simple exploits of norms and groupthink through creative social engineering. The famous skeptic Richard Dawkins featured Brown in a documentary series, *The Enemies of Reason*. In his appearance, Brown famously debunked cold reading, a psychological technique used by those claiming to be psychics or mediums. He shed further light on this in his book, *Tricks of the Mind*. His prolific output of books includes titles on magic for practitioners, the general public, as well as on the history of the philosophy of happiness. By deliberately exposing scams and acts of deception, Brown also informs his audience on how to avoid them.

The researcher and author Dean Radin, who directs the Institute of Noetic Sciences, believes that magic is real and can be investigated by scientific methods. He investigates phenomena like telepathy, clairvoyance, precognition, and psychokinesis. All of these fall under the broad discipline known as parapsychology. He contends that these are the areas where "real magic" is manifested and can be studied. But he also acknowledges that serious scientists avoid parapsychology "as though it's a virulent strain of a zombie plague". His view is that only bias and prejudice keep skeptics from accepting the evidence for psychic phenomena like extra sensory perception or psychokinesis. However, he has refrained from claiming the paranormal prize as he maintains that the prize amount will not even cover the expenses to demonstrate the types of psi effects observed in the laboratory. Skeptics like James Randi and Penn and Teller generally consider such claims to be bunk, and worth debunking. Alternative viewpoints like Radin's need to be examined at least to understand the mystical appeal of magic, if not to challenge and scientifically verify many of the fabulous claims. Also, it is worth noting that one of history's most famous, albeit hidden alchemists, was also one of its most well-known scientists, Sir Isaac Newton. During his lifetime, Newton amassed the largest collection on alchemy of his time, and carried out secret experiments away from the prying eyes of the church or the public. This aspect of Newton was largely hidden until the 1930s. It was only when the Nobel laureate and economist John Maynard Keynes bought a collection of Newton's old papers and notes that this neglected part of his legacy was discovered. While this does not mean that Newton somehow also discovered the alchemical philosopher's stone, it shows the degree to which the occult played a role even among "mainstream" thinkers of the time. This trend continued during and after the Enlightenment, along with studies and projects devoted to investigating esotericism and Mesmerism. At the turn of the century, the elite and super secretive group, the Hermetic Order of the Golden Dawn continued studies into occult topics like astrology, divination and astral projection, attracting famous adherents like the poet W.B. Yeats. These efforts led up all the way to the forerunners of stage and performance magic like Robert-Houdin, who himself investigated claims of clairvoyance; and to the growing interest in Spiritualism during the Industrial Age. Even today, distinguished scientists including some Nobel Prize winners, often express their personal belief that paranormal phenomena are believable and also compatible with scientific knowledge. While such claimants are in the minority, and their beliefs are still not considered part of traditional science, they can still make an impact on the public thanks to their stature and reach.

The array of subjects covered by *Penn and Teller BS* show is an interesting and volatile mix that covers everything from religion, the paranormal, medical scams, to alien abductions and extra sensory perception. It reflects both Penn and Teller's innate curiosity and diverse interests, and also their willingness to take a stance based on their libertarian views. The show went on to achieve global success, and was carried by networks in over 16 countries. This would also represent the transition where Penn and Teller evolved from being an American brand to a global brand. They were recipients of the 2001 Hugh M. Hefner First Amendment Award, which was first established to 'honor individuals who have made significant contributions in the vital effort to protect and enhance First Amendment rights for Americans'.

By the end of 2001, Penn and Teller were already in preparation for their next show, which would take them back to the realm of magic. It would re-establish them as major performers, and provide an entirely different kind of platform for a different kind of aspirant.

The Fool Us Phenomenon:
The Show Concept

The British network ITV commissioned Penn and Teller's Fool Us in February 2001. After a positive initial reception, it was announced that a further eight episodes would be produced in a short ten-day filming block beginning in June 2011. As avid viewers know, the format of Fool Us has been highly standardized right from the very beginning. After an introduction to the show and hosts, Penn and Teller make their entrance from center stage and find their way to their seats facing the stage. Thus they cross over to the "audience's side". Like any audience member attending a magic performance, they both want to be tricked and entertained, but also want to be clever enough to crack the magician's code. A series of performers are then introduced by the host or hostess (Jonathan Ross or Allison Hennigan depending on the season of the show), and their sole purpose at that point is to fool Penn and Teller and claim their Fool Us trophy. Like the audience, Penn and Teller see the trick only once, though in some cases the performer may have invited them up on stage for a close-up trick.

At the end of each performance, while they are talking to the host, Penn and Teller attempt to decode the trick from their seats. Given that Teller maintains his silence throughout, Penn has to do all of the talking. He has to communicate the secret of the trick back to the performer without leading the audience in on the specific method. This is mainly done to "keep the magic alive", and let the performer use the trick in their future repertoire. However, Penn Jillette likes to speak in code so that aspiring magicians can always decipher what he is saying if they take the trouble of following his clues. He targets his comments at the younger versions of Penn and Teller who are out there watching. In an interview, he has gone as far as saying that his comments are all "keyword searches". On one level, the comments are cryptic and secretive, and on the other, they can be the pathway to learning more about the tricks in question. On the odd occasion, Teller is dispatched to the stage with a drawing or sketch that communicates their theory to the magician. In a vast majority of these cases, Penn and Teller have cracked the trick. Interestingly however, not all performers who appear on the show expect to fool them in the first place. In many cases, especially when magicians are performing established tricks with slight variations, the focus is more on the entertainment value, and the performers themselves are there to have a good time and get more exposure. But when Penn and Teller get baffled by a trick, it is fun to watch them getting frustrated, angry, or agitated trying to decode it. And of course, there are those rare cases where parts of the trick are known but the performance is so extraordinary that they simply give up and just sit back and enjoy the show. In later seasons, performances by magicians such as Shin Lim, Richard Turner and Ryan Hayashi elicited such a response–it was clear that Penn and teller were just awestruck and you could see the childish wonder especially with Teller. When it came to the legendary blind card mechanic, Richard Turner, Teller was ready to give him the trophy even without waiting for the end of the act. Some routines can be so well-done and overwhelming that even hardened pros can sit back and simply enjoy the show.

Just in case there is a dispute, there is a judge backstage (Johnny Thompson) who has examined to each trick and can step in to verify that the magician is indeed fooled Penn and Teller, and convey this to the host. After each individual performance, if the performer fools Penn and Teller, they not only win the Fool Us trophy, but also a win a five-star trip to Las Vegas to perform as the opening act in their show at the Rio Hotel & Casino. As a final parting gift to the audience, Penn and Teller then come out and perform a trick of their own. For most magicians, many of whom have not performed in such a large venue, being on the show or winning the trophy is a godsend and could indeed change their performing career. As for Penn and Teller, they continue their reign as the longest running headlining show in Las Vegas.

Seasons 1 and 2:
Jonathan Ross and the British Invasion

Season 1 of the show focused primarily on British magicians, given the setting in the UK. Jonathan Ross was chosen as the host for this season. With an extensive and established background as a television and radio presenter, as well as an actor and comedian, Ross was already one of BBC's highest paid stars by 2006. Known for his wit and flamboyant sense of dress, Ross played the role as a smooth master of ceremonies, always ready with a joke, and never overpowering either the magicians or Penn and Teller. He also served as an excellent conduit to the primarily British audience, interjecting the proceedings as appropriate with a topical joke.

It is appropriate that the first season of Penn and Teller: Fool Us, started off in the UK. England in particular, has had a long historical association with magic, and its history and cultural identity have been closely linked to magic since Neolithic times. The charisma and stage presence we associate with successful magicians may have precedent in English history. John Dee, who happened to be an astrologer, mathematician and occultist consultant to Queen

Elizabeth I was perhaps the most interesting examples of the cult of personality. In his prime, he successfully straddled the boundaries of science, magic, religion and politics, and was a lightning rod for his contemporaries. Literary scholars believe that Shakespeare may have modeled his character Prospero in the Tempest after Dee. In more recent times, several British writers have made magic a part of the cultural conversation in the mainstream. These include J.R.R. Tolkien, C.S. Lewis, J.K. Rowling and Neil Gaiman. And the UK has also produced the likes of Dynamo and Derren Brown, who are among the most successful magicians performing today, and prodigious talents like Ben Hanlin, Megan Knowles-Bacon, and Troy Von Scheibner, to name a few.

Similar to Penn and Teller's Fool Us in the US, one of the popular shows in the UK, Magician Impossible, was pioneered by the magician Dynamo. Known also as Steven Frayne, Dynamo is a classic example of a magician who used hustle and street smarts to find his way into the orbit of big name performers. Originally from Bradford, UK, his original start in magic was to protect himself against bullies in the neighborhood, and soon he developed a reputation for skilled sleight of hand. Part of his appeal is the story of social mobility, after a childhood spent in tough neighborhoods, and battling Crohn's disease, to making it in the celebrity culture later in life. After moving to London, he set about creating a mix-tape of performances where he would impress doormen and tour managers to make his way to celebrities and do close-up magic for them. Similar to David Blaine, he used their reactions to serve as promotional material for his skills, and was soon appearing alongside stars like Jay Z, Coldplay, Russell Brand, Ashton Kutcher and Will Smith. In 2013, he won the Virgin Media Awards, despite stiff competition from shows like Sherlock Holmes, Downton Abbey, and Homeland. This win established him as a high-profile entertainer, and soon he was performing as a successful touring magician. His TV Show, Dynamo: Magician Impossible, combines small and intimate performances along with large scale events, and mostly sticks to the format of a field documentary. Ranging from locations like his native Bradford, to London, the show also travels to exotic locations like Miami Beach, the Austrian Alps and Little Havana. Similar in some sense to David Blaine, Frayne achieves an interesting mix of 'real' people off the street, to an intriguing mix of celebrities who constitute his fan. In his acts, besides conveying the routine, the camera always focuses on the reaction of audiences to his tricks. Their astonishment and disbelief is captured dramatically to demonstrate the effect of his magic in an everyday setting. In a renewed version of the Magician Impossible show in 2012, the emphasis was on starting with small scale acts, all building up to a large-scale spectacle in public. In a memorable illusion created for the show, Dynamo walks across the Thames, close to the Houses of Parliament in London. The tension builds up gradually, from the time spectators gather at the start, to their witnessing of the act itself, and then on to their reactions afterward. The camera dutifully captures the worry and anxiety on the faces of the spectators, and eventually to their relief, shock and disbelief later. This mix of emotion makes for powerful television, and Frayne has been able to successfully master the act of public performance made for TV.

Season One of *Penn and Teller: Fool Us* revolved around British performers, many of whom were card manipulators or close up acts, while Season Two lineup included a number of international performers. Popular performers in this season included Nick Einhorn, a mentalist, Michael Vincent, a close-up stage magician and card expert, and Shawn Farquhar, also a close-up performer from Canada, and the former FISM winner in Close Up Magic, and Past President of the International Brotherhood of Magicians. Farquhar not only managed to fool Penn and Teller on his first appearance, but returned later to Las Vegas to do it again. In the second appearance, in a routine titled Sheer Luck, he seemingly recalled randomly selected pages from The Adventures of Sherlock Holmes. He thus became the first magician to achieve the honor of fooling them twice on the show.

One of the more accomplished and highly respected close-up magicians in the UK is Michael Vincent. A three-time winner of the Magic Circle Close-Up Magician of the Year award, Vincent's card handling and presentation are a masterclass in how a magician can astonish a small or large audience with nothing more than a pack of cards. Vincent is also a passionate lecturer and teacher, and the range and depth of his repertoire are inspired from his study of a long line of close-up magicians, and apprenticeships with some (like Slydini). In his lectures, he describes the years of practice and study starting at a very young age; and being inspired by the work and publications of Marlo, Slydini, Vernon, Ortiz, and other greats. While Vincent's tricks did not fool Penn and Teller in his two appearances on *Fool Us*, as they are also familiar with many of the same sources, their admiration of his skill and presentation were obvious. The more fascinating aspect of Vincent to me is his grasp of communication and presentation skills, and how he effectively deploys them during his routines. He had to go the extra mile to overcome a physical disability as well. In 2011, he suddenly lost his hearing. He had to completely recalibrate his approach, starting with training himself how to lip read. He not just an accomplished magician, but also has the ability to inspire people with his own story. It is no wonder then that he coaches everyone from police chiefs to business managers in the art of communication using magic tricks and effects for demonstration. He is also an admirer of the presentation style of Steve Jobs, who knew how to build up expectations, drill down to the key points, and keep his presentation simple and memorable, and always deliver the goods.

The audiences for Season 1 and 2 in the US consistently ranged between 1.5 million to around 2 million. By season 5, the audiences were down to the sub 1.5 million range but the more loyal fans tended to get their quick fix of Penn and Teller through venues like YouTube. Of course, Penn and Teller completely encourage this as we will explore later in the book. Magicians in general are loathe to give away their trade secrets. Penn and Teller have come in for criticism in the past by other magicians for giving away secrets of some popular tricks, including the famous "cup and balls" routine. However, this is becoming more common as a large number of magicians join the bandwagon, especially on social media and online mediums like YouTube, Twitter and Instagram. A casual glance at YouTube reveals a number of them divulging the secrets of popular magic tricks, including their own, in an attempt to build an audience, peddle courses and programs, and build a stronger engagement with the audience. While you could argue that while Penn and Teller were one of the first to realize the potential of being open with their audience and sharing a few insights, others are doing it far more openly and without any regrets. Also, with platforms like YouTube in particular, anytime a new routine is posted online, the comments section below the video almost certainly has an educated and almost precise guess of how the trick was done.

Retaining the Creative Edge

Despite the changing demands over the years, Penn and Teller have managed to retain their creative edge. In an interview with the Harvard Business Review, Penn was quite candid about how they did it. Once a week, he gets together with Teller at a coffee shop, open up their laptops, and throw around multiple ideas for magic tricks. Then they knock down each other's ideas without any compunctions, this ensuring that only the best ideas survive and make it to the next stage. This is classic brainstorming followed concurrently by an iterative new product development process. This has also been described as a form of toggling between their roles as creators and critics. By constantly switching between these two perspectives, they avoid the trap of quickly discounting new ideas without giving it enough time to evolve. They also encourage each other to solve each other's problem, and through this process of create-criticize, they are able to reconcile the big picture question as well as come up with solutions to address the nitty-gritty. To do this effectively, there has to be complete trust between the two parties, and a willingness to acknowledge the weaknesses of one's methods. It could also be that two is the ideal number for such an intense form of back and forth vetting. In larger group settings, things could quickly get out of control, or not be as effective due to the complexity of the interactions.

In the next stage, they take that polished thought that has survived, and begin to embellish it, frequently adding add humor to it, or looking at it from a silly angle. This also gives them insights on how to hide elements they do not want revealed, and gives them the ability to perfect its presentation, and thus its marketability. In addition to their own back and forth while developing new routines, they also use the services of the veteran magician Johnny Thomson, to further fine tune the final performances or add tweaks they may have missed. When asked point blank, in an interview with Forbes magazine, Penn revealed the secret to success. Essentially it boils down to working really hard on things that most people would not put in the same kind of effort for. This belief that the work they do is critical, as well as the ability to put in tremendous amount of time and effort to achieve their goals, has been critical to Penn and Teller's ability to confound their critics, and entertain their audiences. As we shall see, this ability to constantly work on imperfect routines, with incremental innovation and persistence of long periods of time seems to be a hallmark of many successful performers. In Chapter 5, I break down some of the components of their success strategies.

Season 3-5:
Alyson Hannigan and the Move to Las Vegas

Season 3 of Fool Us brought Penn and Teller to the US and to the capital of entertainment, Las Vegas. All episodes were filmed in Las Vegas at the Rio Hotel and Casino. The following seasons (4-5) were also filmed at the same venue and the show was recently renewed for Season 6.

Best known for her role in the television series Buffy the Vampire Slayer, Alyson Hannigan has been the host of *Fool Us* since 2016. While her role is to introduce the magicians as well as debrief them after their acts, she has frequently found herself being called on to assist or participate during their performances. She is also the perfect volunteer for many routines, displaying a mix of hesitation, nervousness, and surprise that brings a human dimension to her participation. This has led to a number of funny moments, both intentional and unintentional, and has cemented her relationship with the audience.

The magician Kostya Kimlat gives a fascinating inside view of his experience performing on Fool Us on his blog. Every though each act on Penn and Teller lasts only around 5-7 minutes, performers arrive much earlier in Las Vegas and spend 3 days beforehand preparing. On the first day, they recorded a bio-package, which includes a shot of the trick being performed. Each team is assigned a personal producer, in the case of Kimlat it was the producer Guy Toam and cameraman Jay Sharron. This video package is used as a promo for the act, and can be seen right before the performance in the finished show. On the second day, Kimlat met with Michael Close and Johnny Thompson, two professional magic consultants who are tasked with understanding each contestant's trick and evaluating if Penn and Teller have correctly guessed the mechanism on the show. Of course, Johnny Thompson is a revered name for magicians, and there is complete trust in his role as an independent expert. The producers of the show, Andrew Golder and Lincoln Hiatt, then provided performance tips to Kimlat so that they can further polish up routines. Knowing Penn and Teller's liking for close-up magic, when deciding on a table arrangement, Kimlat wanted to be as close as possible to them so that the cameras could capture their reactions.

All the episodes for the season are recorded in two weeks, in no particular order. They are then spliced together with editing in post to create a longer episode. Penn and Teller are not allowed to see the rehearsals, so stand-ins take their place. Finally filming begins after day 3. One interesting observation you might have made related to the above is that Penn, Teller and Alyson Hannigan wear the same outfits throughout each season. The reason for this is simple, given the performances being recorded in bulk, thus giving the editors the option options to select the sequence of routines into each show episode as they see fit. Thus, what you may be seeing in an aired episode may in fact be a selection of acts from different recording sessions.

Though an appearance on Fool Us gives magicians between five and eight minutes to wrap up their performances, that time can literally change their lives, especially if they managed to fool Penn and Teller, but also if they were able to deliver a unique and memorable performance. A successful performance on *Penn and Teller: Fool Us* is not only a badge of honor; it also gives magicians (both professionals and unknown amateurs) the ability to build new connections, reach a global audience, and create greater buzz and awareness among potential clients. As we have seen earlier, a number of performers who have appeared on the show have seen their careers literally transformed by the experience. Shin Lim, Ryan Hayashi, Vinny Grosso, Kostya Kimlat, and others have described how simply getting a chance to perform on the show is a great motivator, and in turn has pushed them to work hard on making their performances unique and memorable.

While the format of the show would suggest that Fool Us is a talent show, Penn and Teller are very vehement that it is anything but. They have professed their intense dislike for talent shows on television, mainly because the judges in these shows may not be the most qualified. They may also miss out on judging breakthrough talents simply because they are too novel or different. Hence, when they set up Fool Us, they made it a point never to be judgmental about magic acts on their show, or give any comments about the future business potential of performers. The sole criteria for judging acts would be whether at that point in time, they managed to fool the duo. Thus, Penn and Teller in their roles are not judges per se, but rather we can think of them as subject matter experts who get one chance to unravel the trick that was performed. This creates a level playing field for all performers, and keeps the game interesting for the audience as well. They also particularly enjoy the interactions with the magicians after the show, where their guests frequently share new riffs and compare notes. Some of these backstage interviews are posted on YouTube, where fans can keep track of the proceedings. Penn Jillette likens this to musicians sharing and comparing riffs with other musicians, which can be a fun way of learning new things from your peers. This also creates the sense for the participating magicians that despite the intense rivalries, they are all part of a professional community, where camaraderie and fun can be as important as the competition.

Chapter 5:
Key Success Lessons

"Magic is a very economical way to amaze people. All you do is deftly lie with your body or with your words. It doesn't require large pieces of scenery or choruses of naked people in feathers. If you keep your overheads low, you can survive even in hard times."

—Teller

"I think that if you worry about staying on the cutting edge, you're less likely to stumble onto it. To have any chance at innovation, you have to start with passion."

—Penn Jillette

Creativity and seeking new challenges

Jillette believes that the key to an entertaining performance can be either passion or sheer technical expertise. In his experience, he says he has rarely seen both in the same person, but that is the lofty goal to aim for. In the book, *How to Persuade People Who Don't Want to Be Persuaded*, the authors reveal how persuaders over the generations have used carefully develop skills to convert the staunchest disbeliever. Among their key attributes: a narrow focus, understanding the decision process in the brain of the person whom you're trying to persuade, being able to read tells and other involuntary giveaways, extreme persistence (and optimism), creating an emotional bond which the audience, personalized attention (knowing your subject's name really helps here), and a belief that no challenge is too difficult to conquer. Successful magicians have mastered most if not all of these techniques, and they deliver their routines with smoothness and precision. Penn and Teller always have put artistic success over financial success. By not compromising on their artistic values and interests, they made sure that their acts retained their integrity. This approach has also allowed them to maintain their creative output over a long period of time, and remain true to their roots as creators of magic in addition to being leading exponents of the craft.

Teller has always had an interest in theater, and co-directed a production of Shakespeare's Macbeth, first at the Folger Shakespeare Theater in Washington D.C, followed by a run at The Yard at Chicago Shakespeare Theater. This production, described as a supernatural horror thriller, was extremely well received, for the way it was conceived, and the impact of its special effects, derived mainly from magic adaptations by Teller. Teller and the director Aaron Posner stayed true to the script–this meant making apparitions appearing out of cauldrons, as well as daggers floating in thin air, just as described in the original play. While the idea of using magic special effects in theater is now new, there is a revival underway. Magicians are once again getting more opportunities to perform theatrical and narrative magic in films and plays. This enables new works to build characters and narratives, and magicians work with the directors and costume designers as a part of the development team. Teller has collaborated with director Aaron Posner to incorporate magic into two renewals of Shakespeare work, *The Tempest*, whose magical landscape lends itself very well to such an intervention. Nathan Allen, director of the House Theatre of Chicago's *Death and Harry Houdini*, has said that a well-executed magic trick can unite audiences in their amazement. This show recreates several of Houdini's signature acts in an intimate theater setting, with a small cast of seven. Allen wanted the magic in the show to be a social experience, and has found that it can work particularly well in small venues where the audience feels they are part of a select group. This also increases the intimacy between viewers and the recreated Houdini stunts that are performed on stage. Allen plans the stunts based on the size of the room they are performing in, and the actor who plays Houdini, magician Dennis Watkins, has to plan how to make it happen. The stage tricks often have to be redesigned to fit into smaller rooms with up-close audiences. In the early days, the budget for the production was very low before successful shows started increasing the operating budget, giving more latitude to the production team. Several acts were added and cut to fit the narrative theme of the show. For example, producing doves was nixed because it did not add to the story, while a scene about Houdini witnessing his father being sawed in half was added. Both Allen and San Francisco performer Christian Cagigal aim to use magic to further a narrative and build an emotional response during storytelling. Cagigal's aim is to make magic to storytelling what song is to theatre, a medium for development, and an important accessory to the enjoyment of the performance. There is a big difference between an individual magician putting on a parlor magic act, versus a collaborative theatrical production that relies on a team of talent. It goes without saying that the latter requires more teamwork and collaboration, but it also gives performers to fine tune the scale and complexity of the production, whether it is delivered in an intimate theater setting, or in a large entertainment venue with thousands of seats.

One of the most popular illusions ever conceived, was first used in a stage production of the Charles Dickens story, *The Haunted Man*. This clever optical illusion, developed at the Polytechnic in London in the 1860s (now called the Royal Polytechnic Institution), was named "Pepper's Ghost". A three-dimensional, ghost like figure would appear on stage, with an ability to move and glide through solid objects. Unknown to the audience, there existed another room adjacent to the stage, and the actions taking place in it were then projected onto the stage using the right placement of a clean sheet of glass. In the case of Pepper's ghost, this room happened to be below the stage, but it can also work with the room on the same level situated at the correct angle. This effect observed is similar to our experience when we see the contents of the room we are in reflected in the window glass, while at the same time seeing the scene outside the window itself. This is because glass can both reflect and transmit light under some conditions. The underlying technique is used to this day and can be seen at the Haunted Mansion exhibit as well as in an appearance of the Blue Fairy in Pinocchio's Daring Journey at Disneyland in Anaheim, California. When Pepper's Ghost was at its prime at the Polytechnic, it was a sensation and attracted a steady stream of visitors.

Pepper's Ghost Effect
(Reproduced from "Illusions optique," *Le Magasin* (1869): 284.)

The Polytechnic was established in 1838 as a private company with the objective of disseminating scientific and technological knowledge by displaying the underlying architecture and mechanics of the objects and technologies on display. It was known for its Magic Lantern exhibitions, a type of projection technique that was one of the predecessors of the modern-day slide projector. People would come from far and wide to enjoy such an exhibition, a far contrast to today where one can view more advanced wonders sitting at home. One of its earlier inventions, the Sphinx, also enjoyed widespread success. A small box was typically carried on stage, and placed on a table. Soon, a head wearing an Egyptian headdress appeared on the table. This Sphinx would then smile, look around and answer questions. The effect was on the spectators was one of shock and amazement. The simple contraption relied on mirrors underneath the table, which cleverly concealed the Sphinx's lower body, thereby creating a convincing illusion of a dismembered head on the table. One viewer hypothesized that the Sphinx's voice was being piped in from a different room, whereas the head, he believed, had obviously been decapitated, and would not survive more than a few minutes. Pepper's Ghost used a more elaborate effect which required considerable prior preparation and proper installation and testing. The Polytechnic became a noted venue where audiences went to get educated about the technological marvels of their age, and could ponder the workings of everything from photographic flashes, to early models of typewriters, telephones and microphones.

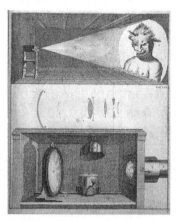

A Magic Lantern projecting a monster
(Reproduced from *Physices Elementa Mathematica*,
published by Willem Gravesande in 1720.)

Similar to the Polytechnic, Paris was the site of the Boulevard du Temple in the 1860s, the destination to go to for magic shows, the viewing of ghostly visions accomplished through optical illusions, and expositions on science and physics. Founded by Henri Robin, this 'scientific theater' would introduce audiences to the latest developments in various fields including archaeology, geology and astronomy. Following the tradition of the Théâtre-Robert-Houdin established in the 1840s, the Boulevard du Temple cleverly blended the boundaries of science and magic, and drew in crowds attracted to the 'mysterious and the marvelous'. Through these efforts, developments in magic in both London and Paris led to the popularizing of science and technology, even if the boundaries between the real and the fantastical were somewhat blurred for the cause of public entertainment. Throughout the nineteenth century, magic thus contributed to the urban fabric, and the magician's trade was accorded importance and respect.

In recent decades, the tendency to incorporate magical thinking has spilled over from drama and theater to corporate America as well, particularly in the area of creating unique customer experiences. The challenge for service based businesses in particular is the need to create inspired and creative products and services that are completely new, but feel completely natural and obvious to a first-time novice user. This is similar to the idea of a magician spending years perfecting a trick, but when the audience sees it, it looks so natural that you cannot see the sweat equity that has gone into perfecting it over time. As the creativity coach Aran Rees points out, if the creative product feels effortless, audiences may undervalue it. But smart companies like Apple and Disney are able to use showmanship and razzle-dazzle to create a feeling of awe and astonishment; thereby creating the necessary conditions for their customers to pay premium prices for their seemingly effortless but extremely creative offerings. Service oriented businesses in particular are paying renewed attention to showmanship, and by extension, the art of magic, in order to create experiences that delight their customers. This is because the customer experience is at the center of their business model, rather than the physical premises and infrastructure or the core product itself. It is no coincidence that one of Disney's premier properties is called the Magic Kingdom, and carries the added tagline, 'The Most Magical Place on Earth'.

Persistence pays, especially if you are obsessive

The field of magic is a fertile ground for people who are extraordinarily persistent and are able to overcome adversities. There are famous examples like the Argentinian magician René Lavand, who became one of the leading exponents in Europe despite losing one hand in a childhood accident; Matthias Buchinger, born without hands or feet, but went on to become the 'Greatest German Living', to, in our own time, Richard Turner, who can "see" all the cards he is dealing despite being legally blind. Turner, a self-described card mechanic, is barred from all casinos as he would literally break the house. Watch one of his performances to contemplate the deep mysteries of human talent and abilities. Turner's fingers are so sensitive that they can detect moisture levels in cards that computers routinely miss. He is on retainer with The United States Playing Card Company, who sends him samples of their playing card decks for testing; in exchange for his services, they send him all the cards he wants. In a classic motivational talk combined with card magic show, he recently took on an auditorium full of smart MIT students and left most of them slack jawed. In addition, Turner is a sought after motivational speaker and a fifth-degree black belt despite his handicap. Mahdi Gilbert, a Canadian magician born without hands or feet, appeared on the third season of *Penn & Teller: Fool Us*. His performance of the card trick *Oil and Water*, won him the coveted Fool Us trophy and a trip to Las Vegas. Gilbert states that there are no magic books written for him, therefore he took it upon himself to create tricks that he could perform. And then there are those like David Copperfield who have the audacity to dream up ambitious stunts like making the Statue of Liberty disappear or walking through the Great Wall of China — and then go on to make it happen. In a similar vein, the popular Indian magician P.C. Sorcar made the Taj Mahal vanish using an optical illusion. When asked if he was a scientist in order to be able to pull of such a feat, he calmly replied, "Science and magic are the same". A day in the life of a hardworking magician.

Penn and Teller may have a smaller budget than Copperfield, but they are no slackers themselves. Penn, for example, has stated that he does not want to retire to a standard routine and "play golf"; but rather would like to continually develop new material. Teller is even more meticulous and obstinate, and will go to extraordinary lengths to make a trick happen. For an appearance on David Letterman, Teller started by putting on a series of tricks involving a top hat that failed to impress the host (by design). For the grand finale, he managed to drop the hat unceremoniously on Letterman's table, revealing 500 live cockroaches that were soon sent crawling all over his "workspace". In order to pull this effect off, Teller put in months of preparation, including hiring an entomologist who could help them make the cockroaches move slower than usual, and who also taught him how they could be handled without getting squeamish. They then built a secret foam core partition into the top hat–the material being one of the few that the insects cannot cling to, thus forcing all of them to land on the table. The shock value (for Letterman and the studio audience) made it all worth it. Magicians will go to any length to create an unforgettable impact. David Copperfield has stated how he spends up to five years (and a lot of money) to perfect just one effect, constantly working on it till it is ready for the stage. The efforts taken by David Blaine to perfect his endurance tricks are legend. This seems to be a common feature among successful professional magicians, where they simply do not abandon their efforts in developing a better effect, in some cases for decades, whether it is for surmounting a physical barrier or simply creating a more mystifying experience for their audience.

Another great example of doggedness is displayed in Teller's performance of the Red Ball trick. The routine starts with Penn announcing to the audience that it is just a trick done with a thread. An effect adapted from a floating ball trick proposed by David Abbott, Teller manipulates a red ball around the stage, which seemingly acts on his command. Teller spent nearly eleven months perfecting this trick, and realized it might be novel to do a floating ball trick for a ball that does not float. On the suggestion of Johnny Thompson, the balloon was given a personality, like that of an obedient dog. That humanizes the performance, and successfully creates an emotional bond with the audience even though no words are spoken. In the actual performance on the show, Penn ends the trick by cutting the thread on stage and revealing the trick. The effect of this trick is still stunning, even with the knowledge that the ball may be controlled by a thread. In fact, the beauty of the trick is that it doesn't matter even if you know the method, a well-executed trick can still fool the mind as long as the story and presentation are close to perfect.

As Teller explained it in an interview with The American Life, it is impossible to evaluate a magic trick if it is half-finished. It needs to be perfect before you can tell if it is good or not, unlike in other arts where mistakes or imperfections can be easily hidden. As he states succinctly, "Magic is a fantastically meticulous form...magic is an on/off switch. Either it looks like a miracle or it's stupid." One lesson from this approach is even during the process of prototyping, product developers can stretch their abilities to the max, and come up with not just another iteration, but something that is fundamentally new. By aiming for perfection at each of the stages, the likelihood of a "perfect" or near-perfect product at the end will increase. This notion also applied to personal communication and presentation skills. A finished presentation where all the kinks have been ironed out through revision and practice is much more dramatic and effective than one that is still a work in progress. The practice sessions can happen either solo, or with close friends or colleagues, until it is ready for prime time in front of a larger group. The key to success in both these cases is preparation and practice, and taking the time to make small but continuous improvements throughout the process. When the final product is delivered or the final presentation is made, it will then have a better chance of looking both perfect and effortless. Here's how surprise works.

When it comes to persistence and single minded pursuit of an objective, David Blaine's approach to breaking an endurance record offers several insights. For many of his performances, he spends months if not years in training, while experimenting with new techniques that can help him achieve his objectives. In a fascinating TED talk, he reveals how he trained for an endurance attempt involving the longest breath-hold. As a child with asthma and no physical advantages, he learnt from a very young age to push his endurance to prove to himself that he could compete with his more athletic friends. After grueling experiments on his own body, multiple blackouts where he needed to be revived by medical professionals, and public failures, he continued on his quest. Through his extreme (and some would say fanatic) dedication, Blaine is able to surmount physical pain, humiliation, rejection and failure, while keeping his eye on the prize. Blaine ultimately broke the Guinness World Record for holding his breath underwater, with a time of 17 minutes and 4.5 seconds, in an appearance on the Oprah Winfrey Show. In true Blaine style, he also obsessively prepared for the TED talk itself, locking himself up in a hotel room while composing and rewriting his notes on a deck of playing cards.

Ability to look beyond the immediate

Many artists and performers, especially after an early success, tend to take the easy way out, either by not continuing to push their own personal boundaries or that of their profession, or by getting used to the trappings of their success. Penn and Teller have been ahead of their time in predicting future trends and societal changes. They have done this by investing in their craft and practice, not taking easy shortcuts, and by not compromising their exacting standards. They have also remained steadfastly focused on their magic rather than on the material rewards that may result from it. To use a business analogy, they have been extremely diligent at focusing on the immediate projects that need their attention for day-to-day success, as well as considering new opportunities in the pipeline that may lead to higher growth. Doing both of these well also enables them to invest in seeding the new opportunities that will sustain their future franchise. As Geoffrey Moore, author of the business bestseller, *Crossing the Chasm*, points out, "Like good farmers, managers see that they must simultaneously harvest the current crop, till the ground for next season, and investigate new crops for the future". Whether it is managers in organizations, or magicians seeking to build a long-term career for themselves, the lessons seem to be universally applicable. This approach a strong belief in lifelong learning, and the willingness to constantly re-examine one's assumptions, while making ongoing improvements to technique and presentation.

Emerging magicians today are faced with a Catch-22 situation: while they encounter greater challenges in establishing themselves in the pantheon of great performers, they also have the ability to harness innovations that most performers of the past could have only dreamed of. The ability to study and devour training in the form of lectures and videos from the world over at the click of a button, the chance to reach out and interact with a global audience while fine tuning their capabilities, and getting near instantaneous feedback and encouragement from peers and fans are all abilities that they can and should tap into. This can also help them create a brand, increase awareness about their performances, and possibly open up new market opportunities both in the physical or digital realms. To the self-promotion part of their skills set, they can now add video editing, podcasts, social media, and viral marketing. Of course, some of these skills can also be outsourced to third parties depending on the size of the business, but for a lot of professional magicians who start out as solo entrepreneurs, a lot of it is based on a personal investment of time and effort. These have all now become essential skills they need to master towards their own personal success. This is no different than any other area of endeavor where entrepreneurs are trying to make their mark, but in the case of magic it is made more poignant as it starts with just one person and their unique vision.

The magician Joshua Jay emphasizes that magicians who are starting out should first focus on magic before worrying about the business prospects. He believes they need to spend at least ten years perfecting their craft, making it the singular focus, and only when truly singular skills and material have been developed, should they think about marketing or building a brand. However, he sees a lot of younger magicians today thinking only of their brand, focusing intensely on social media likes and followers rather than spending the time on taking their craft to the next level. Part of the reason for this may be that that there is tremendous pressure to keep pace with what is perceived to be the best practice, and newer entrants do not want to be left behind. In his experience, Jay says that the most monetarily successful magicians he knows, without exception, are those who spend a lot less time thinking about marketing, and a lot more time focused on how they can improve their craft and push themselves artistically.

Mastering Control and Improvisation

There are many routines in magic that are classified as 'self-working'. Used typically in in card magic, mentalism or mathematical tricks, the production of effects depends purely on following a standard process, and can be repeated by any audience member. These self-working tricks require no special skill on the part of the magician; they are essentially fail-proof. Optical illusions, certain scientific effects, and number tricks also fall into this category. The audience ends up discovering a unique feature of a natural phenomenon, or discovering an effect that is always true but was previously unknown to them. A classic example of a self-working card trick is the "Magical 13" routine. A spectator is asked to cut a deck of cards 13 times, and the deck is then split into 13 different piles. When these piles are examined, it is found that each of them contain cards of the same value. While astonishing, this is a completely natural principle. If the deck is originally set up like a fresh pack with all the suits in order, this is a self-working trick as the cards always end up thirteen places away from each other, thus separating themselves into piles of like valued cards.

However, most routines in performance magic are not self-working, but involve the skill and intervention of the performer. These require not just complete knowledge of the underlying tricks, but the ability to execute them successfully. Successful magicians thus have another characteristic that they tend to perfect over years of practice: they are extremely good at switching between the modes of complete control, and emergency improvisation. These are the two contradicting ends of the spectrum that a magician has to constantly deal with, whether in close-up performances, or in delivering a show to a large audience. On the one hand, it goes without saying that they need to be able to control all the critical aspects of the tricks they are performing, and this ability is acquired through constant experimentation, training and practice, and years of experience performing the routine. But almost every trick has some element that could potentially go wrong, causing it to be ill executed, resulting in an embarrassment at the minimum or an outright failure in the worst-case scenario. Magicians are aware of the tension that exists between having complete control while giving the impression that the performance itself is effortless. In order to prevent or at least minimize the possibility of such failure, they also need to know how to improvise their way out of sticky situations. Frequently, tricks can have multiple outs, in the sense that at least part of the effect can be salvaged by choosing an alternate route in the event of a glitch. This is where their own self-confidence, prior anticipation and practice, and rapport with the audience play a critical role. In the case of Penn and Teller, their strong interaction with the audience, and the ability to explain away any problems through humor play a major role in helping them retain control of their presentation. In the case of David Blaine, there are several instances where he has had to improvise and react to changes during the performance. For example, an audience member may misunderstand the instructions during a card trick, or not remember a selected card, forcing the magician to come up with an alternate ending. The ability to think quickly on one's feet is thus a valuable quality for every magician.

Willingness to open up the platform and recognize others

The success of Fool Us clearly demonstrates Penn and Teller's ability to open up their platform to all comers, thus inspiring the average amateur to hardened professionals to their show. Why is this important? Penn and Teller, unlike other acts in Las Vegas, have created an entertainment platform for new talent. Every other show in town is focused solely on the individual performer on the marquee. By contrast, Penn and Teller's show is more egalitarian. They have reached a stage where they do not need to prove themselves anymore in the eyes of their audience, or their peers for that matter. Ryan Hayashi describes them as the "grand gentlemen of magic" who have taken it upon themselves to spread the gospel of magic through their efforts. Through this unique platform, they are connecting audiences to stars that would not have otherwise drawn any attention. They have also created new stars simply by giving them an equal opportunity to perform on their stage. In a humorous exchange during Shin Lim's follow-up appearance on Fool Us, for example, Penn mentions how fans accosting them at airports seem more interested in talking about Lim, rather than Penn and Teller. Established magicians can now reinforce their connection with a global audience, while new magicians can be discovered. As we have seen before, in some cases, a single appearance on Fool Us has dramatically altered the trajectory of the performers career.

The Magic Castle, which we have referred to before, is a mandatory stopping point for any aspiring magician and magic aficionado. Magicians go there to learn, perform, and be entertained by their peers. Established in 1963 as a private club in Los Angeles, the Castle boasted regulars like Cary Grant, Orson Welles and Johnny Carson. Despite a slowdown in business thanks to the increasing prominence of special effects in film, the fortunes of the Magic Castle improved after the actor Neil Patrick Harris took over as the President in 2008. All visitors to the Magic Castle must whisper a password to a sculpture of an owl to gain entry. It represents club magic in a formal, classic setting. There are several venues within where magicians can perform: The Close-up Gallery, The Parlor of Prestidigitation, and a large stage in the Palace of Mystery.

It also boasts a séance room and a piano played by a ghost, which takes requests. It is also a restaurant with multiple bars scattered throughout. A long list of impressive performers held court there, starting with the sleight-of-hand expert Dai Vernon. Jason Alexander, who played George Costanza on Seinfeld, performed there for a week to much acclaim, though he put his career in magic on hold and switched to acting. Interestingly, the vast majority of the performers have been male, but that could change with the increasing success of female performers in the field. As an institution, the Magic Castle has had an outsize impact on the evolution of the field. It has provided a sanctuary to members of the magic community, whether to recharge themselves, learn new tricks and techniques, or in showcasing their efforts to their peers and an appreciative audience. For members of the public, it holds a certain allure. In order to gain entry into this world, you would have to know a member, communicate ahead of time with a magician who will perform there, become a member oneself, or use your wallet to stay at the hotel and buy a souvenir photo. And of course, if you do manage to get in, you definitely need to be attired formally. Very recently, the Magic Castle started posting recordings of performances online, and these have been very successful with a global audience.

Magicians have long relied on platforms and communities like the Magic Castle to exchange knowledge, and also improve their skills. They realize the benefits of sharing their knowledge in exchange for learning a new technique or trick that they might have been unaware of. In any field where there is a need for novelty and innovation, it is inevitable that such platforms (either open or semi-open) are created and sustained. We have the romantic image of the lone inventor poring over a problem before coming up with a new idea, but the reality is that innovation is usually a shared pursuit, and breakthroughs usually happen when there is a sufficiently shared body of knowledge. As the popularity and reach of magic increases, the platforms themselves are undergoing rapid change. Shows like *Penn and Teller Fool Us*, and the *Got Talent* franchise seem to have been the early drivers and beneficiaries of the trend, but it is likely that there will be more venues where such talents can be showcased. Another important aspect to consider across all these forums is the ability for magicians to test out their ideas with real audiences. This ability to constantly get feedback in real time from actual viewers or customers is very important when it comes to improving the effects being presented. It also gives them the ability to polish their presentation and delivery through such repeated interaction. Similar to a neutral university setting, it is also a valuable opportunity for experts to transfer some of their knowledge to new students and professionals, thus ensuring the continuity of the discipline.

Promoting magic and inspiring young people

A number of performers on the Fool Us explicitly mention how watching a Penn and Teller performance early in their lives, or watching them perform on TV, had a lasting impact on their lives. Some of them were inspired enough to make magic their calling, and have spent the rest of their lives improving their skills as they become professional magicians. One of the magicians who recalls being inspired by Penn and Teller is Kostya Kimlat, who fooled them with an elaborate card trick which left Penn fuming. He then proceeded to give Kostya the best compliment one magician can give another, "I hate you!". Like Penn and Teller, Kostya, a talented performer who mainly works business audiences, has a theory about why magic can be so inspiring, especially to younger people, and perhaps also to jaded adults. By learning magic, he believes one develops a number of skills that can help in our daily lives. These include: looking at a problem from a slightly different point of view, ability to speak and present to an audience, and physical skills like dexterity and hand-eye coordination. Armed with these newfound skills, one can then literally "open one's eyes" to new possibilities. Magic in particular has a great capacity to inspire young minds, especially once they discover that they can perform some basic tricks with some practice. And once the spark is lit, there are plenty of freely available resources to continue the quest.

In blog posts documenting his visit to Las Vegas, Kostya Kimlat provides a terrific insider view of the process of appearing on Fool Us. On the day of the performance, he casually mentions to Johnny Thompson, the legendary magician whose invitation brought him to perform, that he spent the previous afternoon touring Siegfried and Roy's Secret Garden and Dolphin Habitat, Thompson casually asks, "And did you meet Siegfried?". Turns out that not only did Kostya meet him, but also had a long conversation with him and ended up with an autograph as well. Magicians seem to have a natural affinity to hang around, and talk to their audiences in formal and informal settings. Through the process, they are constantly learning, teaching, and building a rapport with their fans.

Penn and Teller have discovered an interesting venue to accomplish their goal of bringing magic into people's lives: merchandising! They have developed a magic trick kit for purchase that includes effects that can be performed by aspiring magicians of all ages. They frequently give away prize kits on their TV show as well. Produced exclusively for them by Royal Magic of Chicago, this USA-made kit includes simple tricks like the Ball Vase, and complex ones like the Penetration Frame, that can easily fool a roomful of adults. In a play on words, it is labeled "Fool Everyone". This is another way for them to reach out to their audience, and also inspire a new generation of aspiring magicians. Other magicians who have also taken this road include Criss Angel and Jim Stott.

Ability to scale without sacrificing original identity and style

The individual style and personalities of Penn and Teller define who they are, and what they want us to perceive them to be. Throughout their long and successful career, they have not lost sight of this fact and kept their image and brand very consistent. Although the formats and venues where they appear have changed, their spirit of innovation, their preference for a good joke, and their ability to communicate (with or without speaking) has remained unchanged, and in fact has gone from strength to strength. This ability to maintain brand identity despite the scaling up of their operation, their business research and audience size is critical to their long-term success. Their audience reacts to this instinctively, and follows them with sincerity and enthusiasm. Despite the fact that the duo has performed together for so long, theirs is a completely professional relationship. When they get together for a performance, it is all business. While they turn to each other for friendly advice, they do not socialize outside of work.

As Jillette has gleefully observed, the biggest illusion they have been able to pull off is that they are a two-man show. Their business is driven by a dedicated team, some of whom have been with them for decades, starting as young as 18. The show is run by Kathleen Boyette, and their business manager is Glenn Alai. They manage all the decisions related to operations, logistics, marketing, human resources. This includes the logistics and details associated with their shows, TV appearances, and travel. Being based at the Rio Hotel in Vegas, some of the logistics have been simplified, but Penn and Teller still occasionally tour within the US to locations like Atlantic City and Florida. Another person they rely on is Johnny Thomson, now in his eighties, who has been with them for a long time. Described as a brilliant magic mind, he offers frank and unvarnished criticism, which Penn and Teller take with complete seriousness, given that he has seen it all. Thompson also advises other leading magicians including David Copperfield and Criss Angel. He also serves as an impartial judge in case of disputes between Penn and Teller, and they trust his decisions and instinct completely. Thus, they are able to place their trust in a dedicated team while they focus on the core competence which defines their business—the ability to find new ideas to test and develop into magic tricks. They have not lost this singular focus throughout their long careers.

Perfecting the Business Model

Magicians can take lessons from their counterparts in the music business when it comes to further building a dedicated fan base, both in terms of acquisition and retention, but they are rapidly catching up in terms of best practices. Top music artists like U2, The Beatles, Neil Young and others started the trend of direct interaction with fans and encouraging the creation of communities of fans who could provide feedback as well as become part of a larger group of peers. This trend has been continued by stars like Taylor Swift, Beyoncé, and Rihanna, enabling them to sell out entire seasons in advance, as well as promote related merchandise or exclusive experiences. We see a similar trend among the top names in magic, given the substantial revenues from repeat customers, their dedicated fans. Penn and Teller, for example, believe that audiences should be able to interact with them for free. To this day, after nearly four decades of performances, they saunter out after their shows to meet audience members, sign autographs, and pose for pictures, without charging a dime. However, this is a dying trend, and several performers realize that there may be big bucks to be made by monetizing these opportunities. In recent years, David Blaine has been one of the standouts in terms of adopting such a model to further enhance fan experiences, which in turn lead to higher revenues. For example, VIP packages that include the ability for fans to meet and greet with top performers typically cost over five times the regular ticket price, but loyal fans are willing to pay and line up for the unique experience. These packages reveal the imaginative use of utilizing the performers time, and monetizing every single aspect, before, during and after the show (See Table below). It also allows Blaine to get the most bang for the buck for each show; resulting in him having to perform less during the course of a typical year, but performing with full intensity on the days of the show. This is particularly important in his case, as many of the tricks he relies on require a lot of preparation and a strong stomach (especially if it has to also serve as a mobile aquarium holding live frogs and fish).

Front Row VIP Meet & Greet Package for David Blaine's Show

- One premium reserved ticket in the Front Row!
- Individual M&G and photo opportunity with David Blaine!
- Watch David Blaine perform card tricks in an intimate setting before the show!
- Pre-show hospitality with drinks and light snacks, including cash bar with 1 drink ticket (where available)
- One signed deck of cards
- One specially designed show poster
- VIP meet & greet laminate
- Exclusive VIP tote bag
- Pre-show merchandise shopping opportunity
- Designated VIP Nation check-in
- On-site VIP host

There are several strategies employed by performers to achieve their business goals. These deal with everything from creating awareness, reaching out to and engaging with fans, creating unique user experiences, exclusive benefits for premium customers, and also expanding their global reach. Some of the commonly employed models used by leading magicians to achieve these business objectives along with sample activities in each category, are listed below. By focusing on specific aspects of the underlying business model, they can deliver key benefits along each of the identified focus areas.

1. Focusing on Platform Expansion: As part of this strategy the idea is to use the core brand and intellectual property, and expand to new channels of distribution to increase sales revenues. Third parties can also be used to facilitate this expansion. A good example would be magicians using TV shows and spot appearances to generate interest and drive traffic and sales to their live shows, or to simply create more awareness of their brand. The creation of such platforms can also lead to eventual peer-to-peer communication between customers and community formation, if managed correctly.

2. Focusing on Targeting: The idea here is to understand construct profiles of customers based on several dimensions. These could include demographic, psychographic, and lifestyle variables that can be collected with market research. This information can be used to create memorable and compelling experiences for customers who are thus profiled, ensuring that their needs are met better. This, in turn, can lead to higher levels of customer satisfaction, loyalty, and repeat purchases.

3. Focus on Transactions: Here the goal is to close the loop between user engagement and potential commerce activities. These could include merchandising, special promotions for fan clubs, and other activities that increase the likelihood of transactions. Transactions are particularly appealing when the encounters between performer and customer are sporadic or one-time, but the ideal situation would be to convert these individual transactions into long-term relationships.

4. Create membership experiences: This involves taking transactions to the next level, and involves building a meaningful relationship with the customer through carefully constructed experiences. Here the idea is to further refine the targeted audience to a core group of dedicated users who are willing to pay for unique services, like through a membership program. A great example is the method used by David Blaine's sales team to develop special packages that deliver on the entire experience. This can include items like the show, hotel stays, pre- and post-show experiences, opportunities to meet with the performer, and other cross marketing opportunities. These types of experiences can reinforce the central branding message, and create more satisfied and loyal customers over the long run.

5. Focus on globalization: Here the focus is on creating opportunities in new geographic markets, particularly overseas. This could be much harder for individual performers unless they are willing to spend time on tour. In the world of magic, this idea can work better for ensemble acts. For example, The Illusionists perform with a rotating cast of magicians in several overseas locations. Benefits include an expanded market, brand recognition, and ability to draw on a wide diversity of audiences. The downside is that this can result in a challenging lifestyle involving constant travel.

Chapter 6:
Conclusions

If you like the stuff I do, my chances of liking you go up.
—Penn Jillette

Doing beautiful things is its own reward.
—Teller

A Business and Cultural Phenomenon

Penn and Teller, like the profession they represent, are a business and cultural phenomenon. Instantly recognized, with a brand that stretches from the US to far flung corners of the globe, they represent how an evergreen brand can ride the wave of the entertainment business. They are a ubiquitous presence not just in Vegas or on TV, but also on social media, and video sharing sites like YouTube. This has helped them bridge communication barriers and continually attract new audiences. They also exemplify how magic itself has become part of the popular culture. As Lev Grossman, who writes for TIME Magazine, and is the author of The Magician's Land, points out, magic and fantasy have replaced science fiction as popular escapes for the post-Internet generation. C.S. Lewis and J.R.R. Tolkien, creators of the fantasies *The Chronicles of Narnia* and *The Lord of the Rings* published their books in the 1950's, and were part of a generation that went through the wars and had seen the world undergo tremendous social, physical and technological transformation. To reclaim the lost world they grew up in, they created unique and vibrant fantasies. These fantasy worlds, often with elaborate structures and set of rules, were a compensation for the chaos and change in the real worlds they inhabited. In recent decades, the birth of the Internet and the information revolution that followed has completely altered the storytelling landscape. We have changed in terms of how we think of the era before the Internet, and there are of course large numbers of consumers today who are simply unaware how things were before the instant connectivity and access to information. It is almost as if we are characters in this fantasy world of bits and atoms, using technologies to connect with people far and wide, but at the same time also ignoring people in the same room. The millennial generation, for example, simply takes this for granted. Magic offers us an escape from our new world, which itself is composed of things that are seemingly magical. By presiding over a show like *Fool Us*, Penn and Teller now serve as gatekeepers, filters, and custodians of magical talent, and serve a critical function in how magic shapes popular culture. Other successful magicians like David Copperfield, David Blaine, Dynamo, and others, through their own unique style and focus, are contributing to the continued success of magic performance.

Changes in the world of magic have to be seen over the long arc, recognizing the social, cultural, economic and technological changes that accompany the passage of time. Jillette cites the example of the 1895 silent film, *The Arrival of a Train at La Ciotat Station*, which runs for 50-seconds and simply shows a train pulling into a Paris station. It is said to have caused terror in the audience and many of them jumped out of the way. Nobody had seen such an effect before, and it caught them totally by surprise. However, a fraction of a second later, nobody was fooled by it anymore when they realized the absurdity of the situation. Jillette points out that this kind of trends have continued to the present day. With television becoming an integral part of our lives, we pay scant attention to ads anymore, as we are so conditioned to decipher the intent behind the commercial. Similarly, he believes that the

Internet is starting to reach the same kind of leveling off, where people will be able to distinguish between the good and the bad, and the genuine from the fake. As Jillette exclaims, "The whole idea that everybody else is going crazy on the internet sickens me. I can tell when something is garbage. You can tell. Who are all these mysterious people that can't?" He is of course alluding to the era of fake news and alternate realities which get amplified in the echo chamber of today's social media. His bigger point is that broad cultural changes take time, but the directionality of the change should be pretty clear to an astute observer. Further, the art of magic automatically adjusts to the changes in society. Though it can be argued that the vast majority of magic tricks and effects are based on age-old principles, newer magicians will push the boundaries further in order to create delight and wonder. By using multimedia technology and devices, special props and gizmos that were previously unavailable or too expensive or complicated to construct, and engaging their audiences in unexpected ways, they will attempt to create new effects that mystify and bamboozle. This can also be a lucrative market segment to target for magicians with a mechanical bent. A successful magician who has carved out a niche in the area of creating magic effects that can be purchased and used by fellow magicians is Jay Sankey. Sankey, a Canadian close-up magician, is also a stand-up comedian and the author of *Zen and the Art of Stand-Up Comedy*. He has developed special effects that have been used by magicians like David Copperfield and Criss Angel, and also written authoritative books on coin magic. Boasting more than three hundred and forty-six thousand followers on YouTube, Sankey is a prolific producer of videos which demonstrate his knowledge of magic. Like Sankey, some of the performers on *Fool Us* and on the *Got Talent* franchise are already exploring these boundaries. Irrespective of the amount of technology they bring into their acts, they will be following in the footsteps of magicians before them who have always challenged the status quo as they drive the art forward. They will still need the simplicity, directness and expert presentation to continue wowing audiences.

Meanwhile, magic is entering the political domain as much as the economic and cultural ones. In an interesting development,

Representative Pete Sessions (R) of Texas recently submitted a bill to Congress to make magic a national treasure on the grounds of it being a "rare and valuable art form." (full text of the bill in Appendix 1). The resolution recognizes the benefits and economic impacts of magic. These include references to the technological contributions of prominent magicians, the social and economic impacts of famous magicians like David Copperfield and Harry Houdini (Copperfield has started Project Magic, aimed at helping disabled children with magic), and the entertainment factor of magic being on par with other forms of non-written expression. The resolution concludes by calling for appropriate conservation measures to promote magic as a national treasure. Since the sixties, The Society of American Magicians has been pushing Congress to recognize magic as an art form, and this bill is the latest manifestation. As pointed out earlier, New York City mayor Bill de Blasio has designated October 6th as "Chamber Magic Day" (full text of the mayoral resolution in Appendix 2). Several such initiatives are underway in other states which are dependent on tourism, and where the entertainment business, of which magic is a part, is a key driver of their service based economies. These examples clearly illustrate the broad cultural, social, and economic impacts of magic. The days of it being relegated to circus sideshows is long gone; rather, it is becoming an integral part of the national conversation. Cities and states around the country and the globe are recognizing that magic is a critical component of the entertainment economy and can be an attractive draw to tourists and residents, and have a positive economic impact on communities.

Penn and Teller's decades of experience in performing magic to a wide variety of audiences has also attracted academic attention. They have collaborated with academics including psychologists and neuroscientists to test out theories of perception, memory, and other constructs in controlled experimental settings. They have lectured and performed at institutions like Oxford University and the Smithsonian Institution, and were recognized as Visiting Scholars at MIT. Through their efforts, they continue to push the boundaries on the possibilities of magic, and getting experts from other disciplines involved in examining the age-old practices of magicians.

Expanding the size of the market

Shows like *Penn and Teller: Fool Us* and the *Got Talent* franchise have given the opportunity to a host of new performers to reach out to entirely new audiences and demonstrate their mastery of magic. Through this, they are also turning consumers into an educated audience, and discerning consumers of magic. By promoting completely unknown performers, they are expanding the size of the market and bringing in a lot more consumers who might otherwise have not been interested in magic shows or performances. Despite being a characteristically American brand with growing international appeal, Penn and Teller have created a unique spot for themselves both in Las Vegas as well as the rest of the globe. More recent seasons of the *Fool Us* show have included performers from all over the globe, including several from Europe, Asia and Latin America. Magic truly has a universal appeal despite some of the stylistic differences in how it is practices in different countries, and does not always need words to create an impact (Teller may be on to something). This also makes it very easy to sell and convey to a TV audience, who can now feel like they are part of the audience in the theater while the actual trick is performed. Similarly, on the Got Talent franchise, there is a steady flow of performers who cross international barriers. For example, in a recent episode of Britain's Got Talent, there were performers from the US, Japan, South Korea and Malaysia. After an outcry by British audiences about this preponderance of international performers on BGT, a spokesperson for the show had to issue a statement clarifying their position. In their view, the fact that so many international performers are auditioning for the show was testament to the international success of past British acts such as Susan Boyle and Paul Potts. Many of these performers realize that a breakthrough on such a popular platform could mean a big change for their careers, and are willing to travel to great distances in order to prove their worth.

Another sign of market expansion is the growth in the number of solo women performers, which has been a rarity until recently in the world of magic. In the 1880s, Madame Adelaide Herrmann broke into the world of magic by taking the place of the traditional boy assistant, and creating the tradition of the glamorous female partner or assistant. Others soon followed, including Bess Houdini and

Dot Robinson. Madame Hermann, after the death of her magician husband, took the unusual step of taking on the lead role of the Queen of Magic. Despite this early breakthrough, female magicians still continued as sidekicks to their magician partners. The most famous of these was Charlotte Pendragon, who performed in a duo with her husband for many years as The Pendragons. Penn Jillette has mentioned in an interview that he is impressed by the number of women magicians coming in to perform, both on *Fool Us*, and in general. He thinks that the boy's club image of magic is crumbling, and within a decade, there will be several women who dominate the magic scene. The tradition of women magicians in the West is sparse, in contrast to the situation in Asia and Eastern Europe. This can be attributed to historical factors; there was a time when you could literally be burnt at the stake for practicing the 'black arts'. In Asia, women practiced magic as parlor entertainers, and there were no real barriers. Instead, it was even considered a high art form and attracted talented and wealthy women. Out of the six solo female magicians who appeared on *Fool Us*, five of them managed to fool the duo; a very high success rate. Jillette attributes this to the fact that the way solo women think about magic is completely different, and they have not been conditioned by the boy's club way of thinking. He points out that their unique styles and nuances are very alien to magicians who grew up in an industry traditionally dominated by male magicians, who also formed secret magic societies that kept women out for a long period of time. Jillette not only finds the new trend refreshing, but considers it a very encouraging and much needed development for the future of the industry. In one of the *Fool Us* episodes, Penn and Teller insisted on getting women magicians to perform one of their old acts; their choice was the pair of Jen Kramer and AmberLynn Walker, who went on to perform a flawless routine. Jen Kramer, for example, represents the new type of talent making an appearance on the national scene: a Yale theater graduate, she had previously served as the Founder and President of the Yale Magic Society, and taken up a career in magic. Jillette's own daughter, Moxie Crimefighter, is an aspiring magician, and has appeared in a surprise cameo with David Garrard on *Fool Us*. Jillette believes that within a decade or so, the major forces in magic will be women, and there will be a number of superstar entertainers among them. As more women magicians enter the field, there will also be a natural expansion of the market as well.

Implications for other businesses

The domain of business is no stranger to developments in magic. In fact, especially in fields like marketing, which has a strong interest in understanding and using persuasion, considerable debate exists about the role of magic and magical thinking. As Chris Miles, a researcher at the Queen Mary University of London succinctly puts it, marketing scholars have been arguing for a while that advertising works like magic in that it blinds consumers to the "real" nature of the world. Instead, it employs themes and idioms associated more with the world of magic and witchcraft. Business journals and periodicals are replete with words like transformation, enchantment, glamor, spells, incantations and the much-used ingredient X (the 'secret ingredient', or the X-factor). Similarly, the continued use of celebrity endorsements suggests that marketers want to encourage magical thinking in consumers, and have them buy products that can somehow confer upon them the gifts and abilities of their stars through the power of association. At the core of the matter is marketer's sensitivity to being labeled bluntly as "persuaders". Persuasion still remains at the core of all dialog and communication, and marketers would be wise to study some of the techniques that magicians deploy in getting their ideas across, rather than completely distancing themselves from the use of persuasive communication.

Besides the areas of advertising and persuasion, the magic industry offers lessons for firms engaged in prototyping, new product development, and the creation of new business opportunities. In today's global service economy, firms are on the constant lookout for products and services that seem 'magical' to consumers, and not just meet but exceed their expectations. If they exceed expectations in this way, they can create customer loyalty, as well as generate free promotion through word of mouth. Handsome dividends can indeed be had by developing such products and services. Like firms with limited resources, magicians are themselves under tight budgets to create new tricks, and need to constantly and systematically innovate to exceed their audience expectations, and also promote themselves effectively. It turns out that magicians are keen practitioners of systematic new product development: they need to have a deep understanding of what needs to be solved, find out how to solve the problem, know when and how to hide the solution, and also sell the experience convincingly. Top notch magicians like David Blaine, Penn and Teller, and David Copperfield, for example, have spent decades fine tuning their craft, and have done the hard work of ideation, experimentation, prototyping, product development, practice and performance, and then done it all over again multiple times. They frequently consult with experts, and in some cases, employ a team of people on stage to help deliver their complex routines. In magic, the notion of top-down innovation involves looking for something fresh and new, while bottom-up innovation involves using an existing trick to draw upon or improve. Both of these modes of discovery can happen in parallel, and usually serendipity plays an important role in making the exact connection. Magicians are fortunate in that they have a massive repository of knowledge that has been painstakingly built up over the years through many iterations. There are multiple authoritative books available on every form of magic that is performed, and knowledge is also transmitted directly from teacher to student, or peer-to-peer. Firms can take inspiration from this and institute top-down development that comes out of a sustained program of research investment, or also look for bottom-up solutions by tweaking existing products, getting feedback from lead users and loyal customers, and also tapping into a larger pool of ideas through venues like crowdsourcing and partnerships. There is a strong need to build a comprehensive repository of knowledge that can be relied on while coming up with new ideas and solutions, rather than reinventing the wheel every time there is a problem.

Often hired by corporate clients to develop entertainment acts, professional magicians must first take the trouble of really understanding what their clients want, and innovate a way to get the client's point across with the wow-factor of a magic trick. Both innovators and magicians need to make a product unique but still mystifying. Some innovators look for top-down innovations when working on a project. This may involve defining the business proposition clearly, and then figuring out the operation details required to deliver it. Virgin Galactic first envisioned what a journey out to space would look and feel like, before working on the operational and logistical details. Presenting a clear concept helped sell out seats on the first few flights, and individual customers were putting down deposits in excess of a quarter of a million dollars each for the experience that lay far in the future. Though founded in 2004, it took nearly fourteen years for them to demonstrate the viability of the concept. In December 2018, Virgin Galactic flew its first astronauts to the edge of space, demonstrating that their original idea was not just wishful thinking. Similarly, Disney focused on building the magical atmosphere of Disneyland before focusing on the technical challenges and the service delivery aspects. Also, not including unnecessary complexity and doing something simply but effectively is a big part of business and magic innovation. Several great examples of this abound, include Apple, Bose Audio, Citibike, or even Tod's Shoes. The idea is to captivate your audience without confusing them, and execute on the promises by delivering a consistent, high quality experience. This requires both clarity of vision, but also the ability to surmount significant hurdles to realize it.

As part of their long heritage of experimentation, professional magicians have developed a detailed process for trick development that can be broken down into three stages. The first is focusing on the 'how's', where they look for a breakthrough where top-down experience meets bottom up processes. To aid this, many magicians they keep a Tech Box to help them with breakthroughs. Hence the term a 'magician's bag of tricks'; a general all-purpose box of odds and ends that can somehow be reconfigured to the needs of the moment. The name of the game is improvisation, re-discovery, recombination and reuse. Firms like P&G have started doing this with their industrial database covering cross disciplinary fields that help facilitate creative cross-connecting. Pharmaceutical firms do it by maintaining and mining a large database of molecules that may help discover the next blockbuster drug. Firms in the Internet sector have massive databases that store information gleaned from customer profiles and behavior over a long period of time. With the advent of tools like machine learning and artificial intelligence, it is now possible to mine this information to discover new trends, and also possible new market opportunities. The explosion of data, including that covering personal profiles and behavior, is creating a war for consumer insights derived from analytics, and a lot of it is taking place invisibly without us even realizing or knowing it. As Kai-Fu Lee, the former President of Google China, points out in his book *AI Superpowers: China, Silicon Valley, and the New World Order*, artificial intelligence is now routinely tracking hundreds of weakly correlated variables to come up with predictions of probable outcomes. In an interesting case of the use of such algorithms, he describes how a low battery level on your phone may be a better predictor of your credit-worthiness than other commonly used indicators. Developments like these can be expected to accelerate as hardware and software capabilities get exponentially better, conferring seemingly magical powers to marketers and influencers. In the entrepreneurial realm, the resource toolbox can include the business model canvas, the lean startup manual, SCRUM (a framework for agile development), and the product design canvas, for instance. By resorting to the use of a toolbox or a techbox, the main benefit is that practitioners do not have to reinvent the wheel every time they encounter a new problem. And with greater use of these tools comes greater familiarity, dexterity and expertise, which allows them to drill down to the solution quickly.

The second step is deciding what and how to hide things. As Professor Stefan Thomke of Harvard Business School points out in his study of magic and business, conducted jointly with the magician Jason Randal, there are two kinds of magicians: "magician's magicians" (those who perform complex tasks) and "audience's magicians" (those who perform easy tasks, but with a huge wow-factor). Audiences don't know how much work goes into the latter, but it takes hours, days and weeks of practice and fine tuning. Different levels of display work for different audiences. Houdini was one magician who kept everything transparent. Besides being impressive to the audience, the effect was also mystifying as they struggled to decode what they were seeing. In business, this approach may work for products where you want consumers to know the innards of the product, and perhaps works better if users are of a technical bent (e.g. programmers or engineers). At the other extreme, hiding everything from the customer can also be an approach that works. For example, as Thomke and Randal describe, Bang & Olufsen, a leading player in the audio industry, keep their user interface very minimal, to avoid complicating things for users, but also sticking to the fundamental design principle of 'less is more'. Similarly, Apple, since its inception, has also relied on minimal design. Steve Jobs drew inspiration from minimal forms of creative expression, including Japanese calligraphy and Zen Buddhism, and was a great admirer of Dieter Rams, the famous German industrial designer. Engineers, like magicians, must know that not showing everything is sometimes beneficial. Magicians must strike the right balance of hidden and shown, and ask what could easily be hidden, what can be revealed or concealed during the trick, and how to hide the real ending. A good example of this is when David Copperfield adapted a trick by removing a concealing element halfway through an illusion, but by then he had changed how the levitation system worked, wowing the audience even more. They expected one thing and got another. Teller mentions how it is critical to captivate an audience's attention and then lead them through a series of twists that eventually helps strengthen the ultimate impact of the routine. This involves precise anticipation of the customer perceptions and making accommodations for every step in the way as they are being guided (or misguided, as the case may be). The third step is selling the performance in such a way that emotionally appeals to the audience. We described earlier how Teller performs simple but extremely effective tricks like Shadows or the Red Ball. Several magicians who appeared on Fool Us commented on how they were inspired by the early Penn and Teller trick involving only a pencil and a cigarette, which they have also helpfully deconstructed to the audience. At the end of the day, simplicity and emotional impact trumps technical wizardry, and also creates a more direct and personal connection with the audience. As Einstein famously said, keep everything as simple as possible, but not simpler. If there is enough passion and conviction and an emotional bond has been created, the audience is willing to forgive or ignore the minor missteps that are bound to happen. In the area of product development and marketing, creative directors and chief designers are often associated with mysterious magical forces that bring together creativity with the power of transformation. This is particularly true of iconic designers of luxury products. John Galliano, Karl Lagerfeld, Dieter Rams, or Jonathan Ive (of Apple fame) are held in high esteem for this ability to envision a new aesthetic despite facing the same material obstacles and constraints as everyone else. Like magicians, they possess transformative intentionality, practice their own form of shape-shifting, and frequently transgress expectations, often taking great risks and displaying enormous amounts of persistence. Anthropologists looking at fashion design, for example, have compared star designers to 'shamans' who can grapple with uncertainty and yet 'foretell the future'. The fashion business, and indeed, much of our modern capitalistic society is permeated with magical agents, spells, and rituals of varying kinds. Just like a successful magician, the creative director or fashion designer who breaks through and channels the *zeitgeist* into creative products and services is celebrated and handsomely rewarded.

There are a number of general business recommendations that apply to both magicians and businesses: innovators must continually innovate, because the novel soon becomes standard; and the standard soon becomes obsolete or irrelevant. From a firm perspective, it therefore becomes very important to reward innovative behavior even if failure happens. This also creates a unique organizational culture and identity, and be much more powerful than a set of written rules. In their research, Thomke and Randal found that a lot of firms fail at the task of problem definition, which is usually the most underrated aspect of the innovation process. Rather than focusing on developing solutions, strategists, managers, engineers, and developers should pay more attention to defining their problem first, and defining it well. And if they excel at this part, they will be able to go beyond customer expectations, delight them, and thus deliver the 'magic'. This needs an organizational culture that encourages preemptive practice and prototyping, helping perfect the products and services it is producing. A better understanding of the three R's prototyping really helps: the ability to be rough, rapid, right (you have to get the important aspects exact, but the rest can be approximate). At the same time, one cannot expect creative ideas to be uniformly manufactured, like in an assembly line. People need time and freedom to deliberate and marinate on their ideas, and come up with something truly creative. Hence the vital importance of allowing employees access to some free time or "personal time" as Google calls it, to work on problems of their own interest. These practices capitalize on employee choices and strengths, builds teamwork and collaborative skills, and also creates a culture of trust within the organization.

New product development teams can further enhance their effectiveness if they are willing to actively switch their points of view during the process itself. Taking a cue from Penn and Teller, one strategy that innovators can employ is to constantly toggle between the roles of creator and critic. Critics may kill a new idea, but they also bring the voice of reason, practicality and feasibility to a project. This helps uncover pain points that really exist but can be improved, but more importantly also eliminates the bad ideas really fast. It can also give insights on other values or aspects that can be added or modify to make a piece of work more complete. While for magician's persistence could mean developing and practicing new routines, like training their by pushing the natural limits in cold resistance or breath holding (e.g. Houdini or David Blaine), for businesses it could mean operating out of their normal environment. It could involve rule-breaking and out of the box thinking, like Criss Angel does when porting stage tricks to the street, which tends to be more impromptu and a harder space to "stage" special effects. As Thomke describes in his study, a good business example of this is a BMW team from Germany that spent 6 months working in isolation in California, completely out of their natural home environment, and spent the time creating unorthodox designs for a new car. As many artists, writers, and creatives know, a change in the immediate physical surroundings prompts creative energies and can lead to new ideas and directions. That is what the BMW team found in a completely new locale cut away from all their familiar anchors. Finally, all innovators know that they have to sell the entire customer experience, rather than one isolated aspect. Magicians nowadays must make more concentrated effects to fool the same audience, and ask highly technical questions before, during and after their performances. Similarly, product designers and engineers need to truly understand the mindset of the customer, and be willing to go the extra mile to separate their offerings from that of their competition. Thus, there are many uncanny similarities between the world of performance magic and that of innovation practiced in modern business enterprises.

What Does the Future Hold?

The Internet has revolutionized how people get to know about magicians, and how they can observe, be entertained and also learn from them. Rich Ferguson is a successful California-based magician who has also achieved tremendous success on YouTube, with over a million followers. His video uploads consist of everything from instructional magic and brain games to elaborate pranks that he stages on unsuspecting passerby. Ferguson thinks that the trend towards democratization of magic is two-sided. On the one hand, he feels that this has 'cheapened' mainstream magic, making it less mysterious and secretive, and simultaneously created a large pool of players who may be conversant with basic aspects of magic but do not have the depth and quality to sustain long term success. This may in fact be detrimental to the prospects of top-line magicians. As he pointed out to me wryly in an e-mail, "Heck, why would someone hire a premium expensive magician like myself when the DJ in the phonebook offers strolling magic for the party as a free add-on!?". On the other hand, he points out that such a big pool means that we will also encounter truly amazing talent that is completely undiscovered. The next superstar may very well be a complete newbie just starting out on YouTube. A quick glance at YouTube or other video sharing sites will reveal hundreds of magic tricks, and in many cases, clear explanations on how they can be performed. While several popular instructors have hundreds of thousands of subscribers, and some even have millions. There are a myriad of magicians and coaches offering their ideas, insights, and detailed instructions on a wide range of effects, and also offering many of the effects and props for sale.

Ferguson considers that he got into magic rather late in life, at the age of twenty-seven. However, once he discovered it, he was hooked. To him, it was an excuse to indulge in his interest of entertaining people, given his knack for body language and personal interaction. Within a few months, he decided he would do it full-time for a living, a major decision at the time. Given his skills in marketing and networking, he soon found the most lucrative gigs by catering to custom, private and VIP events. Not only that, he created his own pricing structure and targeted the premium end of the market, thus ignoring the conventional wisdom in the field. His other interest was catering to everyday people, and develop approachable tricks and pranks—in this quest, he soon discovered the global reach and marketing power of YouTube. His YouTube revenues in 2016 were in excess of three hundred thousand dollars, and since then, he has been on a roll on the platform and not looked back. On his channel, many of his videos garner views in the hundreds of millions. He has also collaborated with other magicians like Jay Sankey, for example, to create material and promotions. As far leveraging YouTube is concerned, his belief is that a channel's revenue, assuming a decent-sized audience, lies in the integration of the product portfolio, custom endorsements, as well as creating licensed content for other platforms. YouTube can be the front end of a funnel that feeds traffic to other destinations, including an online store, exclusive content, or other paid locations. Ferguson is of the opinion that magic is entering an exciting phase where the top magicians are going to get compensated handsomely, in proportion to their reach and impact, as well as their ability to understand and use the emerging channels of reaching their audiences. He thinks it is high time, given that there are hundreds of star athletes, movie stars, and other celebrities making more annually than the tenth highest paid magician.

Thus, for the aspiring magician, there is no shortage of venues from which he or she can build their knowledge and skills. In fact, as we have seen before, star magicians like Shin Lim are mostly self-taught, and have benefited from the availability of information and videos online. Theory11, a website founded by Jonathan Bayme, and which he likens to the iTunes for magic, allows customers to browse for magic tricks they like. If they want to learn how to perform one of the tricks, they can buy full videos offering step-by-step instructions. This includes both the working of the trick itself and how to perform it to the best effect. That is the ongoing challenge for the magic business: selling routines when there are sites like Theory11 or even YouTube videos that often just give secrets away. This is not just restricted to the US but also holds in other markets. In China for example, it has been pointed out that the commoditization of magic starting in the 1930s, and ultimately to its democratization in the modern era, where audiences could pay a small sum to watch skilled performers, we are now in a time when skills and objects can be bought for a price. Keeping secrets (especially proprietary secrets) has been key to how magic works. And yet, we're in an age in which information flows so quickly and openly that that seems like an impossible goal. It places a lot more pressure on the top magicians, who spend a lot of time and money creating proprietary effects. But a lot of times, brilliant magic is more about sheer mastery of timing, execution, and the overall show theme and ambience and presentation skills than any deeply held secrets. The same trick can be performed by different magicians, and can elicit contrasting results. One can be memorable, while the other drops like a lead balloon. Jamy Ian Swiss, the magic historian points out, it is all in the interpretation. He likens it to the many versions of the song "New York, New York" that have been recorded, but there is only the one by Sinatra that is recognized as the gold standard. The artistry and skill of the performer is the critical feature that is hard to replicate despite having all the knowledge in the world at your fingertips. As Swiss has pointed out in his essays, at the end of the day, the secrets of magic are merely theatrical tools, and not the essence of the performance. Of course, it takes an entirely different level of skill, organization, and teamwork to put on an elaborate Las Vegas style show featuring magic, theater, and performance art, versus knowing how to perform a few parlor tricks.

As far as the general field of magic is concerned, most magicians agree that we are living in a time of transition. While social media has certainly changed the game, it still hasn't found complete permanence on our lives. The good news is that the trend seems to favor more direct, one-to-one connections between the magician and his or her fans and followers. The magician Joshua Jay speculates that in the future, the nature of the magic experience itself may be reinvented, with formal shows becoming rarer, and audiences flocking to online platforms to see magic by their favorite performers. He also sees a continuing trend of moving towards close-up magic, whereas more challenges may await stage magicians in general, and illusionists in particular. The venues for big box magic and illusions are diminishing, and despite the presence of a few well known performers specializing in this space, this trend is most likely set to continue.

Giving away or selling magical inventions is not a new phenomenon. Most of the major magicians performing today as well as a legion of aspiring amateurs have visited the Tannen Magic Shop in New York City, and many young enthusiasts have walked away with their first introduction to magic. Founded in 1925, it is a magic institution that contains a cornucopia of magic tricks for sale, which can be bought at the store or through its hefty catalog containing thousands of items and props. Tannen has also been a long-time sponsor to Tannen's Magic Camp, a summer camp for aspiring young magicians that has been held every year since 1974. Among its more famous alumni include David Blaine, David Copperfield and the actor Adrian Brody. The documentary "Magic Camp" presents an inside look at the inner workings of this camp, where young magicians learn about the building blocks of magic, and take classes on topics like Character Development, Intermediate Close-Up, and Advanced Stage Magic. Another NYC institution that catered to magic enthusiasts for a number of decades was the Flosso-Hornman Magic Company. With the feel of a magic museum, this collection of magic memorabilia has had some famous owners including the Martinka Brothers to the most famous magician of them all, Harry Houdini. After the death of its last owner, Jackie Flosso, in 2003, the new owner Ted Bogusta, a young computer consultant at the time, moved the store to the Internet. In its heyday, the store was known for its eclectic collection, including automatons that played chess and did tricks, whistling monkeys, and constant surprises like rabbits jumping out of hats at unexpected moments. Although such classic brick-and-mortar establishments are a dying breed, virtual establishments are popping up to replace them.

Another more contemporary example of this phenomenon is Penguin Magic, which has built its empire on selling tricks for a worldwide audience. Through its online videos where the tricks are demonstrated (but not revealed), Penguin has attracted more than one billion views on YouTube, and is followed by over twelve thousand subscribers. Each of these tricks is reviewed by a professional magician, and to date, over sixteen thousand tricks are available for sale. The genius of Penguin is realizing that the "amateur" market is much more lucrative than the market of professional magicians. While most professional performers are content with a narrow repertoire where they have extreme mastery and experience that can be demonstrated to new audiences, amateurs have the challenge of constantly demonstrating new tricks to an existing audience (usually comprised of a small circle of family and friends). Thus, there is a large and growing market of hungry magicians whom Penguin serves, and in the process they have created a large community of users who constantly feed off each other, through reviews, commentary and discussion, as well as meet-up groups back in the real world. As Seth Godin points out in his book, *This is Marketing*, Penguin Magic exemplifies the impact of a dense interconnected community of users in spurring innovation and engaging in constant reinvention and innovation.

The performers and audiences of Houdini's generation certainly did not have this ability to either get access to or rapidly assimilate such a huge body of knowledge. This ability to access vast amounts of content also comes with a downside; magicians themselves have to constantly innovate to surprise new audiences. They simply cannot afford to be left behind in this competitive era. In parallel, the common public is now exposed to magic in a much bigger way than a few decades ago. Along with exposure to a variety of acts and tricks, they are also getting more discerning and sophisticated. Their appetite for high quality magic is thus undiminished and growing. In addition, today's performers must be exceptional self-promoters. It goes without saying that most of them have a YouTube channel which allows them to build a core base of fans, and the more successful one's work with public relations firms to build a brand presence and a social media strategy. While some naysayers think that these trends point to the eventual demise of magic as entertainment, the reality is that we are entering a new world where magic and its performance are both pervasive and constantly changing. There is a growing base of amateur, semi-professional and professional magicians, and with it, audiences who crave genuine entertainment as well as a break from the drudgery of daily life.

In an essay contemplating the future of magic that David Blaine penned in 2014, he argues many of magic's inherent qualities are timeless. Using emotional engagement to draw in the audience, the mastery of presentation skills, and the willingness to put in hours of experimentation, practice and testing makes magic an art form that keeps reinventing itself. Aspiring magicians soon discover that in addition to their technique, they need to work hard on the traits that will help them endear themselves to the audience. These include personal appearance, stage presence, smoothness of presentation, ability to tell a story, and of course their originality and entertainment value. Sarcasm, humor, and bravado can also work to devastating effect as well, in the right hands and at the right moment. Established magicians rely on a loyal customer base, which means they can perform a relatively narrow repertoire of tricks with some rotation, and still attract steady audiences over time. Not all members of the audience are coming in to figure out the solution of every trick, most of them are there to have a good time and get entertained. Despite the widespread access to information about magic tricks through books, the Internet, and social media, the enthusiasm for the craft has always grown by leaps and bounds, contrary to conventional wisdom. Part of the reason is that magic has always inspired younger generations to take up the craft and innovate continually and create new paradigms as they shatter old ones. It has also inspired experienced magicians with successful careers and track records to pass on their wisdom simply because they love the craft.

Blaine's view is that in our technology-obsessed times, where commentators fret about the future of humans and robots, it is not gadgets and mechanics that matter, but the ability to develop the soft skills involving people, perceptions and relationships. Research in psychology also suggests that belief in magic is a fundamental property of the human mind, and further, engagement in magical thinking can in fact enhance cognitive abilities like perception, creativity and memory. Other magicians have similarly stated that the general public is quite savvy to magic, and magicians must not underestimate the curiosity and intelligence of their audience, but rather build upon the common ground that exists between the performer and observer. The practice of magic is thus becoming democratized, which is in contrast to the time when the magician was removed from the plane of the audience.

Some sociologists sound a cautionary note on the move towards magical thinking in our contemporary celebrity culture driven by reality TV in particular, and the glamorization of spectacle. These commentators have argued that magical thinking is also the currency of a totalitarian culture that controls, manipulates and distracts us from real social and moral problems facing society. We would rather watch an hour of vacuous entertainment on TV rather than learn about social injustice, war and hunger, or climate change, for instance, although those issues may be more relevant for our collective futures. It is up to magic-savvy citizens to keep an eye out for artifice, propaganda, and falsehoods used by everyone from politicians, celebrities, and other influencers by exposing the tricks they are using to achieve their more nefarious objectives. A sound knowledge of the techniques of magic, particularly those involving cause and effect, could indeed serve as a weapon for safeguarding democracy, and advancing rational thinking. As long as magic and magical thinking are seen solely as outlets for creativity and entertainment, without devolving into "mind control" or acting as complete distraction from reality, they will have achieved their objectives.

When one watches a beautifully performed trick like Metamorphosis, without knowing the underlying solution, it is indeed a truly magical experience. When one watches it after knowing the underlying mechanics, we treat it more like an advanced puzzle but still derive some satisfaction from seeing how well it is performed, in terms of speed, technical brilliance, or the overall presentation. In both instances, we cannot resist the inherent pull of the magic itself, even as we are getting more informed and educated as spectators of magic. Given its timeless appeal, and its recent renaissance in popular culture, media and discourse, one could argue that the future of magic is extremely dynamic, bright, and full of unexpected surprises. As we have seen in this book, there is an established market for big-name shows, as well as numerous opportunities for performers at all stages of the value chain. Thanks to blockbuster Las Vegas Shows, exposure on TV through shows like *Fool Us* or *America's Got Talent*, there is a newfound interest among a diverse group of people in magic and its successful performance. Younger generations of magicians are making full use of modern technologies to learn, disseminate, and influence their unique takes on the craft. This bodes well for a future era when attention is sparse, but our minds can still be fooled and entertained by a new breed of magicians.

One should not overlook the importance of Las Vegas in turning magicians into household names, by giving them a global platform for entertainment. Over the years, Las Vegas has diversified the sources of its revenues from gambling to more family oriented and themed experience opportunities, including those for small children; and plans are also underway to bring more professional sports activity to the city. Featuring the Vegas Golden Knights in hockey, the Aces in basketball and the 2020 entry of the Raiders in American Football, Las Vegas will be home to some leading teams, along with a brand-new stadium with a capacity of 65,000 across from the Mandalay Bay Resort and Casino. More than $10bn has been reinvested since 2007 into creating new service opportunities including new restaurants, convention and meeting spaces, entertainment venues and other luxury amenities. It is predicted that by 2020, rooms revenue will outpace revenues from gaming, meaning that new opportunities will be created for shows, food and beverage venues, and other entertainment oriented businesses that cater to the new breed of visitors. This creates new opportunities for established and emerging magic entertainers, who can be a dependable draw for family visitors as well as convention delegates. In the short term, one can expect to see more residencies for magicians who have gained national and international recognition, as well as more venues dedicated to performers. As Teller put it succinctly in an interview, "You can't turn around on a street corner in Vegas without bumping into a magician. A certain kind of momentum seems to have grown up here to where this is the place where magicians come". Proximity to talented magicians, an established network of venues and outlets, and the availability of strategic investors creates more collective value and economic activity in the Las Vegas "magic cluster". The gains made by magic and magicians in Las Vegas will trickle down to other entertainment locations around the globe. In fact, many cities in Asia have started to recognize the importance of magic as being a critical part of the entertainment economy, and are making efforts to incorporate this into tourism and urban planning efforts. Cities that enjoy a steady inflow of tourists, both for business and pleasure, need to consider the attractiveness of having established magicians in residence. Many stars of magic today don't just perform traditional shows, but can also deliver inspiring talks focusing on leadership, communication skills, or collaboration. Convention attendees in particular, could benefit from a blend of such 'edutainment'. The top five cities in the US in terms of convention visitors are Orlando, Washington D.C., Las Vegas, Miami and Chicago. Las Vegas tops all American cities in terms of sheer tourist numbers, and is followed by Los Angeles, Orlando, Anaheim, and Atlanta. The trends towards magic residencies in such cities is likely to continue and grow.

Finally, as for Penn and Teller, in the Summer of 2018, they announced that they would be postponing performances till late August so that Teller could undergo a spinal fusion surgery. This was believed to be from his experiences of hanging out of straitjackets, as well as contorting himself in boxes and other contraptions over the past few decades. After a successful operation in early July, Teller was on the road to recovery. During the same period, Penn Jillette underwent a medically supervised water-only fast to help with his blood pressure. They resumed their stage shows in Fall 2018, and are looking forward performing for many more years in Las Vegas and elsewhere.

Afterword

"All magic is 'Here's a quarter, now it's gone. You're a jerk. Now it's back. You're an idiot. Show's over."

—Jerry Seinfeld

"I am a great admirer of mystery and magic. Look at this life—all mystery and magic."

—Harry Houdini

As we have seen in this book, the world of magic is multi-faceted and inherently dynamic. It has constantly evolved over history and both driven and accommodated social, cultural and technological changes. In an era of sophisticated technologies, and the ability of humans to control and manipulate their living and work environments, magic still harkens back to a time when simple objects and ideas can be imbued with miraculous properties. A look at the history of magic and its variety of characters offers us a lesson in the multiple routes that can lead to success and achievement in what is essentially a niche area of human achievement. In this book, we have mainly examined the field of secular magic. Much of secular magic is trivial in that the underlying methods are mundane and simple upon closer inspection and analysis, and they can be taught, learned and mastered with intense dedication and practice. However, the very fact that is trivial makes it such a potent force for cultural change, as it is both transportable across cultures and languages, and also has tremendous endurance and longevity. Like music, magic can in fact be a type of glue to the global culture, as it serves as a universal language requiring little to no translation.

151

The magical arts and entertainments have shaped culture, media, and economic and societal changes over a long period of time, and there is no sign that they will be diminished in their powers anytime soon.

Whether one is a solo performer catering to a small home audience, a marquee brand on the Las Vegas strip, or part of an international magic ensemble, the routes to success are manifold. Magicians are part of an active, extended and engaged community of practice, with unwritten but implicit rules of participation, collaboration, and knowledge exchange. Seasoned practitioners bring their experience and insights to the table while training new generations of magicians, whether in person, online, or through an extended and evolving body of literature. The training, insights, techniques, and engagement that magicians bring to fruition through their carefully developed acts offer lessons for performers of all kinds, including solo entrepreneurs and large organizations. By adapting some of their practices, businesses can take their own performance to a new level, incorporating creative design and problem solving, persistent experimentation, prototyping and testing, and the use of new techniques to engage and delight their customers. By making these practices a part of the organizational DNA, firms large and small can ensure that the spirit of innovation and experimentation will be self-driven and resilient. However, organizations should realize that most if not all of these skills and attitudes have to be earned through hard practice and field experience, so there are no shortcuts. Once the mindset is more receptive, the work will have to begin.

While some predict gloom and doom when it comes to the future survival of magic, my belief is that we are living through a renaissance of popular magic and its performance. There are real challenges facing the profession in terms of open access to knowledge that was for long known to a small group of practitioners. It is likely that the profession will find new ways will to safeguard proprietary acts where significant research and development investments have been made, without resorting to the courts, while at the same time maintaining the vibrant discussion, exchange and collaboration that has characterized the field in the past. These developments have also created new opportunities as more young performers discover magic, and also get engaged in the process of innovation and knowledge creation themselves. As long as humans retain the capacity for awe and wonder, their fellow magicians will find a way to meet and exceed their expectations. Newer and well-informed audiences, in turn, will be willing to pay top dollar for quality magical entertainment. The peak years of magic performance may still be ahead of us, rather than behind us. While the future destinations remain uncharted, we can be sure that magicians still have a trick or two up their sleeves!

References

1. Alexander, Reed (2017), Meet the magician whose stunning tricks enabled him to build a business worth $20 million," <https://moneyish.com/heart/meet-the-magician-whose-stunning-tricks-enabled-him-to-build-a-business-worth-20-million/> (accessed on 11/4/2018).

2. Ares, Nacho (2017), 'Ancient Egypt: Where Magic was Born', Ancient Egypt, pp. 42-47, April-May.

3. Arnold, Eric, Julien Cayla and Delphine Dion (2017), 'Fetish, Magic, Marketing', Anthropology Today, Vol. 33, No. 2, April.

4. Bailey, Michael (2007), 'The Magic Circle: Performing Magic Through the Ages,' Tempus, October 1.

5. Bailey, Michael (2017), 'Magic: The Basics,' Routledge, August 10.

6. Berg, Madeline (2016), "Down The Rabbit Hole: Inside The Lucrative Business of Local Magicians," <https://www.forbes.com/sites/maddieberg/2016/10/28/down-the-rabbit-hole-inside-the-lucrative-business-of-local-magicians/#32827527579a> (accessed on 11/4/2018).

7. Beard, Allison (2016), "Life's Work: An Interview with Penn Jillette," *Harvard Business Review*, October.

8. Black, Sharon (2003), 'The Magic of Harry Potter: Symbols and Heroes of Fantasy', Children's Literature in Education, Vol. 34, No. 3, September 2003

9. Blaine, David (2014), 'The Future of Magic,' The Economist, November 13th.

10. Blair, Iain (2017), 'Criss Angel Reflects on His Magical Career as He Receives Star on Hollywood Walk of Fame,' Variety, July 20.

11. Brancolini, Janna (2012), 'Abracadabra–Why Copyright Protection for Magic is Not Just An Illusion', Loyola of Los Angeles Entertainment Law Review. Vol. 33 No. 103.

12. Brooker, Jeremy (2007), 'The Polytechnic Ghost: Pepper's Ghost, Metempsychosis and the Magic Lantern at the Royal Polytechnic Institution', Early Popular Visual Culture, Volume 5, Issue 2: Magic and Illusion

13. Brown, Derren (2006). Tricks of the Mind. London: Channel 4 Books.

14. Butler, John (2018), 'How Indian Magic, Illusion in its Highest Art Form, Came to the West and Opened Up New, Mysterious Worlds,' South China Morning Post, July 29.

15. Carr-Gomm, Philip and Richard Heygate (2012), 'The Book of English Magic,' The Overlook Press, October 30.

16. Christopher, Milbourne (1975) Mediums, Mystics & the Occult. Thomas Y. Crowell Co.

17. Cohen, Elliott (2018), 'An Actually Magical Convention,' The Atlantic, August 26.

18. Collins, David J. (2001), 'Magic in the Middle Ages: History and Historiography,' History Compass 9/5 (2011): 410–422, 10.1111/j.1478-0542.2011.00776.x.

19. Cuccinello, Hayley C. (2017), "The World's Highest-Paid Magicians Of 2017: David Copperfield Leads With $61.5 Million," Forbes Editor's Pick, <https://www.forbes.com/sites/hayleycuccinello/2017/10/24/the-worlds-highest-paid-magicians-of-2017-david-copperfield-leads-with-61-5-million/#e92751a322c1> (accessed on 11/4/2018).

20. Cuccinello, Hayley C. (2018), "The World's Highest-Paid Magicians Of 2018", Forbes Editor's Pick, <https://www.forbes.com/sites/hayleycuccinello/2018/11/08/the-worlds-highest-paid-magicians-of-2018/#4104c48f4c64> (accessed on 11/19/2018).

21. Curthoys, Ann (2014), 'The Magic of History: Harry Potter and Historical Consciousness', Agora, Vol. 49, No. 4, November: 23-[31].

22. Dandurand, L. (1999), "A market analysis of the family market in Las Vegas", UNLV Gaming Research & Review Journal, Vol. 4 No. 1, pp. 1-16.

23. During, Simon (2004), Modern Enchantments: The Cultural Power of Secular Magic, Harvard University Press.

24. R. W. Dyson, ed., Augustine of Hippo (1998), The City of God, Cambridge: Cambridge University Press, 1998).

25. The Economist (2017), 'Witches Are Still Hunted In India—and Blinded And Beaten And Killed'. The Economist. 19 October.

26. Erdnase, S. W (1995). The Expert at the Card Table: The Classic Treatise on Card Manipulation (1st Ed. reprint ed.). Mineola, NY: Dover Publications. ISBN 978-0-486-28597-9.

27. Evans-Pritchard, E. E. (1937). Witchcraft, Magic, and Oracles Among the Azande. Oxford: Clarendon Press.

28. Faulks, Philipa (2017), 'The Masonic Magician: The Life and Death of Count Cagliostro and His Egyptian Rite,' Watkins Publishing, July 25.

29. Frazer, James George (2009), 'The Golden Bough: A Study in Magic and Religion: A New Abridgement from the Second and Third Editions, Oxford World's Classics, Reissue Edition, April 15.

30. Freeman, Aleza (2009), 'Revealing the Vegas Magician,' Los Angeles Times, March 15.

31. Gasca, Peter (2016), "Looking for the Next Big Industry? It Just May Be Magic," <https://www.inc.com/peter-gasca/the-next-huge-business-opportunity-magic.html> (accessed on 11/4/2018).

32. Glucklich, Ariel (1997). The End of Magic. Oxford University Press. pp. 32–3.

33. Godin, Seth (2018), 'This Is Marketing: You Can't Be Seen Until You Learn to See', Portfolio, November 13.

34. Gopnik, Adam (2008), 'The Real Work: Modern magic and the Meaning of Life,' The New Yorker, March 17.

35. Green, Adam (2013), 'A Pickpocket's Tale,' The New Yorker, January 7.

36. Grossman, Lev (2014), 'How Magic Conquered Popular Culture,' TIME Magazine, August 19th, URL: http://time.com/lev-grossman-magicians-land-magic-pop-culture, last accessed, November 1, 2018.

37. Harrison, Mark (1989), "New Vaudeville: Variety artists in the contemporary American theater," Doctoral Dissertation, New York University.

38. Hass, Lawrence , 'Life Magic and Staged Magic: A Hidden Intertwining,' in Performing Magic on the Western Stage : From the Eighteenth Century to the Present, Francesca Coppa, Lawrence Hass, James Peck, and J. Peck, eds.

39. Hedges, Chris (2010), Empire of Illusion: The End of Literacy and the Triumph of Spectacle, Nation Books.

40. Heilman, J. (2013), "Las Vegas is all about reinvention", Meetings Today, available at: www.meetingstoday.com/Magazines/ArticleDetails /RegionID/231/ArticleID/21130/ViewAll/True (accessed November 1, 2018).

41. Houlbrook, C. and Armitage, N. 'Introduction: The materiality of the materiality of magic', in Houlbrook, C. and Armitage, N. (eds.) The Materiality of Magic: An artefactual investigation into ritual practices and popular beliefs.Oxford and Philadelphia, Oxbow Books. 1-13.

42. Husband, Andrew (2017), 'Penn Jillette On Four Seasons Of 'Fool Us' And Why The Future Will Be Filled With Female Magicians,' Uproxx, URL: https://uproxx.com/tv/penn-jillette-fool-us-interview/, last accessed: December 5, 2018.

43. Huxley, Aldous (1954), The Doors of Perception, Chatto and Windus.

44. International Brotherhood of Magicians (2018), By-Laws and Sanding Rules, URL: https://www.magician.org/about/rules-and-standing-rules, accessed December 1.

45. Jones, Graham (2011), 'Trade of the Tricks: Inside the Magician's Craft,' The University of California Press, September.

46. Jones, Graham and Lauren Shweder (2003), 'The Performance of Illusion and Illusionary Performatives: Learning the Language of Theatrical Magic,' Journal of Linguistic Anthropology, Vol. 13, No. 1, Special Issue: Anthropology of Visual Communication (June), pp. 51-70.

47. Jones, Jay (2016), 'In Often-Pricey Vegas, Magicians Penn & Teller Continue a Free Tradition,' Los Angeles Times, July 13.

48. Jones, Jonathan (2010). 'A Curse On All Your Paintings: The Secret Magic Of Renaissance Art', The Guardian, November 4.

49. Kahneman, Daniel (2011). Thinking, fast and slow. Farrar, Straus and Giroux, New York, New York, USA.

50. Kalush, William and Larry Sloman (2006), 'The Secret Life Of Houdini: The Making Of America's First Superhero', New York: Atria Books.

51. Kimlat, Kostya, "How Fooling Penn and Teller Changed My Life," <https://www.kostyakimlat.com/blog/how-fooling-penn-teller-changed-my-life> (accessed on 10/31/2018).

52. Kimlat, Kostya, "Why I Performed for Penn & Teller," <https://www.kostyakimlat.com/blog/why-i-performed-for-penn-teller> (accessed on 10/31/2018).

53. Kimlat, Kostya, "How A Magician Prepares for Penn & Teller: Fool Us," <https://www.kostyakimlat.com/blog/preparing-for-penn-teller-fool-us-las-vegas> (accessed on 10/31/2018).

54. Kors, Alan Charles and Edward Peters (2001), Witchcraft in Europe, 400–1700: A Documentary History, 2nd edition. Philadelphia: University of Pennsylvania Press, 41–2.

55. Kuhn, G., Amlani, A., & Rensink, R. (2008), 'Towards a science of magic', Trends in Cognitive Science, 12, 349–354.

56. Lachapelle, Sofie (2009), 'Science On Stage: Amusing Physics And Scientific Wonder At The Nineteenth-century French Theatre', History of Science, xlvii.

57. Lamont, Peter, John M. Henderson, and Tim J. Smith (2010), 'Where Science and Magic Meet: The Illusion of a "Science of Magic"', Review of General Psychology, 14(1), pp.16–21.

58. Lamont, Peter (2013), 'Extraordinary Beliefs: A Historical Approach to a Psychological Problem'.. Cambridge: Cambridge University Press.

59. Lamont, Peter (2006), 'Magician as Conjuror: A Frame Analysis of Victorian Mediums', Early Popular Visual Culture, Vol. 4, No. 1, April 2006, pp. 21–33.

60. Lamont, P. & Wiseman, R. (2005), Magic in Theory: An Introduction to the Theoretical and Psychological Elements of Conjuring, University Of Hertfordshire Press.

61. Lamont, Peter and Jim Steinmeyer (2018), 'The Secret History of Magic: The True Story of the Deceptive Art', TarcherPerigee, July 17.

62. Larson, Erik (2003), 'The Devil in the White City: Murder, Magic, and Madness at the Fair That Changed America', Crown Publishers.

63. Leddington, Jason (2016), 'The Experience of Magic', The Journal of Aesthetics and Art Criticism, 26 July, https://doi.org/10.1111/jaac.12290.

64. Lee, Kai-Fu (2018), 'AI Superpowers: China, Silicon Valley, and the New World Order', Houghton Mifflin Harcourt, September 25.

65. Lewin, Nick (2017), Magic Castle Revisited, Vanish International Magic Magazine, May, Issue 34.

66. Lippman, John (1998), 'Magicians Contend TV Specials Shatter Their Illusions,' The Wall Street Journal, Eastern edition; New York, N.Y., 13 Aug: B1.

67. Loshin, Jacob (2007), 'How Magicians Protect Intellectual Property Without Law, Working Draft, Yale Law School.

68. Luhrmann, Tanya M. (1989) "The Magic of Secrecy." Ethos 17(2): 131–165.

69. Macknik, Stephen L. , Mac King, James Randi, Apollo Robbins, Teller, John Thompson and Susana Martinez-Conde (2008),

'attention And Awareness In Stage Magic: Turning Tricks Into Research,' Nature Reviews–Neuroscience, Vol. 9, November.

70. Marchese, David (2018), 'In Conversation: Penn Jillette,' Vulture Magazine, URL: http://www.vulture.com/2018/08/penn-jillette-in-conversation.html, August 14th, last accessed November 1.

71. McCarthy, Niall (2018), "The World's Highest-Paid Magicians," <https://www.statista.com/chart/13594/the-worlds-highest-paid-magicians/> (accessed on 11/4/2018).

72. McKinley, Jesse (2000), 'Doug Henning, a Superstar Of Illusion, Is Dead at 52', The New York Times.

73. Merrifield, R. 1987. The Archaeology of Ritual and Magic. London, Guild Publishing.

74. Miles, Chris (2013), 'Persuasion, Marketing Communication, and the Metaphor of Magic', European Journal of Marketing, Vol. 47 No. 11/12, 2013, pp. 2002-2019.

75. Miller, Elizabeth L. and Joseph P. Zompetti (2015), "After the Prestige: A Postmodern Analysis of Penn and Teller," Journal of Performance Magic, 3 (1), 3-24.

76. Morrell, Dan (2017), Waltham's Shin Lim could be the biggest name in magic since David Blaine, Globe Magazine, August 24.

77. Moore, Geoffrey (2007), 'To Succeed in the Long Term, Focus on the Middle Term,' Harvard Business Review, July-August.

78. Nardi, Peter M (2006), 'The Reality of Illusion: The Magic Castle in Hollywood,' Contexts, Vol. 5, No. 1 (Winter), pp. 66-69.

79. Okamoto, David (1992), 'Don't Try This at Home: Penn & Teller Frightfully Sophisticated,' Colorado Springs Gazette–Telegraph; Colorado Springs, Colo., May: F1.

80. Ólafsson, Magnús(2018), 'Witchcraft and Sorcery in Iceland,' <https://guidetoiceland.is/history-culture/witchcraft-in-iceland/> (accessed 11/4/2018).

81. Osgood, Charles, and Lee Cowan (2015), 'Penn and Teller are magicians whose sleight of hand is never intended to sleight

the audience of intelligence', CBS News Sunday Morning; New York New York: CQ Roll Call, Jan 25th.

82. Österblom, H., M. Scheffer, F. R. Westley, M. Van Esso, J. Miller, and J. Bascompte. 2015. A Message from Magic to Science: Seeing how the Brain can be Tricked may Strengthen our Thinking. Ecology and Society 20(4):16. http://dx.doi.org/10.5751/ES-07943-200416

83. Owen, Alex (2004), 'The Place of Enchantment: British Occultism and the Culture of the Modern', Chicago: University of Chicago Press.

84. Pang, Laikwan (2007), The Distorting Mirror: Visual Modernity in China, University of Hawai'i Press.

85. Perrottet, Tony (2018), 'A Secret Passageway Into the World's Most Exclusive Magic Club,' The Wall Street Journal, December 19.

86. Petrow, Steven (2018), 'Do You Believe in Magic? I Do', The New York Times, June 28.

87. Pfeiffer, Eric (2018), 'The World's Greatest Card Magician Opens Up About His Biggest Secret', URL: 'https://www.good.is/features/richard-turner-card-magic-blind last accessed December 1.

88. Pollan, Michael (2018), How to Change Your Mind: What the New Science of Psychedelics Teaches Us About Consciousness, Dying, Addiction, Depression and Transcendence, Penguin Press, May 15.

89. Pranzi, Travis (2008), 'Harry Potter & Imagination: The Way Between Two Worlds', Winged Lion Press, LLC. December 10.

90. Priest, Christopher (2005), The Prestige, Tor Books, First Edition.

91. Radin, Dean (2006), 'Entangled Minds: Extrasensory Experiences in a Quantum Reality', Paraview Pocket Books.

92. Radin, Dean (2018), 'Real Magic: Ancient Wisdom, Modern Science, and a Guide to the Secret Power of the Universe,' Harmony; 1st Edition, April 10.

93. Rao, Bharat (2001), 'Broadband Innovation and the Customer Experience Imperative,' International Journal on Media Management, mcm-Institute, University of St. Gallen, Switzerland, Summer 09/2001.

94. Rao, Srinivas (2018), An Audience of One: Reclaiming Creativity for Its Own Sake, Portfolio, August 7.

95. Rees, Aran (2017), "The Value of Magic. And what that means for creativity.," Open for Ideas, January 10, 2017, URL: <http://openforideas.org/blog/2017/01/10/the-value-of-magic-and-what-that-means-for-creativity/> (accessed on 10/31/2018).

96. Rich, Frank (1985), Stage: Penn and Teller, The New York Times, April 19.

97. Ritner, Robert Kriech (1993), 'The Mechanics of Ancient Egyptian Magical Practice,' Doctoral Dissertation, The Oriental Institute, University of Chicago.

98. Ritson, Mark (2003), 'Blaine may be unhinged but he knows a thing or two about PR,' Marketing, p.16, October 2.

99. Schaffer, Simon (1999), "Enlightened Automata", in Clark et al. (Eds), The Sciences in Enlightened Europe, Chicago and London, The University of Chicago Press.

100. Schwabel, Dan (2017), 'David Copperfield: How He Became The World's Most Successful Magician,' Forbes Magazine, available at: https://www.forbes.com/sites/danschawbel/2017/02/08/david-copperfield-how-he-became-the-worlds-most-successful-magician/#1dee77402132 (accessed November 1, 2018).

101. Schwartz, D.G. (2017), "Seven year switch: how Las Vegas hospitality has changed", Vegas Seven, available at: http://vegasseven.com/2017/02/16/seven-year-switch-las-vegas-hospitality-changed/ (accessed November 1, 2018).

102. Scot, Reginald (1584), 'The Discoverie of Witchcraft, Wherein the Lewde Dealing of Witches and Witchmongers is Notablie Detected,' British Library, London.

103. Seligmann, Kurt (2018), 'The Mirror of Magic: A History of Magic in the Western World', Inner Traditions; 6th Edition, October.

104. Sexton, Max (2015), 'Deception Reality: Street Magic from Blaine to Dynamo', Critical Studies in Television, Volume 10, No. 1 (Spring), Manchester University Press, http://dx.doi.org/10.7227/CST.10.1.3.

105. Seymour, St. John D. (1989), Irish Witchcraft and Demonology (Dublin, 1913, repr. London, 1989).

106. Sneddon, Andrew (2015), 'Witchcraft and Magic in Ireland,' Palgrave Macmillan.

107. Sexton, Max (2013), 'Secular Magic and the Moving Image: Mediated Forms and Modes of Reception', Bloomsbury Academic.

108. Sherlock, Jared R. (2015) "The Effects of Exposure on the Ecology of the Magic Industry: Preserving Magic in the Absence of Law," Cybaris: Vol. 6: Iss. 1, Article 2. Available at: http://open.mitchellhamline.edu/cybaris/vol6/iss1/2

109. Silverman, Rachel Emma (2000), 'Houdini's Old Magic Shop Disappears, Reinvents Itself as an Online Retailer,' The Wall Street Journal, December 15.

110. Simon, H. A. 1977. Models of Bounded Rationality, Volume 3: Empirically Grounded Economic Reason. The MIT Press, Cambridge, Massachusetts, USA.

111. Singer, Mark (1987), 'Tannen's Magic Camp,' Grand Street, Vol. 6, No. 2 (Winter), pp. 167-175.

112. Smith, H. (2000). Cleansing the Doors of Perception: The Religious Significance of Entheogenic Plants and Chemicals. Jeremy P. Tarcher/Putnam.

113. Standage, Tom (2002), 'The Turk: The Life and Times of the Famous Eighteenth-Century Chess-Playing Machine', New York: Walker.

114. Staniforth, Nate (2018), 'Here Is Real Magic: A Magician's Search for Wonder in the Modern World,; Bloomsbury USA, January 16.

115. Steinmeyer, Jim (2004), 'Hiding the Elephant: How Magicians Invented the Impossible and Learned to Disappear,' De Capo Press, September 15.

116. Steinmeyer, Jim (2012), The Last Greatest Magician in the World: Howard Thurston Versus Houdini & the Battles of the American Wizards,' TarcherPerigee, August 30.

117. Subbotsky, Eugene (2014), 'The Belief in Magic in the Age of Science,' Sage OPEN, 4(1), January.

118. Swiss, Jamy Ian (2001), Shattering Illusions: Essays on the Ethics, History, and Presentation of Magic Hermetic Books.

119. Tait, Derek (2017), The Great Houdini: His British Tours, Pen and Sword History.

120. Tait, Derek (2018), The Great Illusionists, Pen and Sword History.

121. Thomas, Cyril, Andre Didierjean and Gustav Kuhn (2018), 'the Flushtration Count Illusion: Attribute substitution Tricks Our Interpretation Of A Simple Visual Event Sequence', British Journal of Psychology (2018), 109, 850–861.

122. Thomke, Stefan and Jason Randal (2014), "The Magic of Innovation," The European Business Review, May-June.

123. Thomke, Stefan, and Jason Randal (2012). "Innovation Magic." Harvard Business School Background Note 612-099, May.

124. Tingle, Rory (2018), 'Is This The Most Stomach-churning Magic Trick Ever? David Blaine Sews Up His Mouth With A Needle And Thread Before Cutting It Open To Reveal A Frog On Jimmy Fallon's Show,' The Daily Mail, April 26.

125. Tobacyk, Jerome (2004), 'A Revised Paranormal Belief Scale', International Journal of Transpersonal Studies, Vol 3, Iss. 1.

126. Tompkins, Matthew L. (2018), 'Observations On Invisibility : An Investigation On The Role Of Expectation And Attentional Set On Visual Awareness,' Thesis, Oxford University.

127. Tucker, Cheryl (2008), 'A Tour Through the Pazzi Conspiracy', The Florentine, November 13.

128. Macknik, Stephen L., Susana Martinez-Conde, and Sandra Blakeslee (2010), "Mind over Magic?." Scientific American, Vol. 21, No. 5 (November/December), pp. 22-29.

129. Martinez-Conde, Susana and Stephen L. Macknik (2008), "Magic and the Brain," Scientific American, Vol. 299, No.6 (December), pp. 72-79.

130. Quiroga, Rodrigo Quian (2016), "Magic and Cognitive Neuroscience," Current Biology, 26 (May 23), pp. R390-R394.

131. Taleb, Nassim Nicholas (2007), The Black Swan: The Impact of the Highly Improbable. Random House, New York, New York, USA.

132. Tachibana, Ryo and Hideaki Kawabata (2014), "The Effects of Social Misdirection on Magic Tricks: How Deceived and Undeceived Groups Differ," i-Perception, Vol. 5, pp. 143-146.

133. Thompson, Zac, (2016), "Sleight of Mind," American Theatre, July/August, pp. 26-29.

134. Vollmer, Christopher (2017), "The Revenue Stream Revolution in Entertainment and Media", Strategy+Business, May.

135. Vangkilde, Kasper Tang (2017), Foretelling the future: The fashion designer as shaman', Anthropology Today Vol 33 No 2, April.

136. Vollmer, Christopher (2017), "How to Make Entertainment and Media Businesses 'Fan'-tastic," Strategy+Business, May.

137. Walter, Damien (2012),'Why English Culture Is Bewitched By Magic,' The Guardian, February 23.

138. Williamson, Colin (2015), Hidden in Plain Sight: An Archaeology of Magic and the Cinema, Rutgers University Press.

139. Wiseman, R. & Lamont, P. Unravelling the Indian Ropetrick. Nature 383, 212–213 (1996).

140. Witter, David (2016), 'A Brief, Wondrous History of Chicago Magic', The Chicago Reader, August 26.

141. Zubrzycki, John (2018), 'Jadoowallahs, Jugglers and Jinns: A Magical History of India, Pan Macmillan India, June 28.

142. Zubrzycki, John (2018), 'Empire of Enchantment: The Story of Indian Magic,' C Hurst & Co Publishers Ltd, June 21

About the Author

Bharat Rao is an educator, writer and speaker. He is an Associate Professor in the area of Technology Management and Innovation at New York University's Tandon School of Engineering. He has researched, written, and consulted extensively in the areas of innovation, marketing and technology strategy. An electrical engineer by training, he earned a Ph.D. in Marketing and Strategic Management from the University of Georgia, and was formerly a postdoctoral research associate at Harvard Business School.

Besides magic, he is keenly interested in photography and travel. He lives in New York City.

Appendix 1:
A Magic Bill

Full Text of Bill Proposed by Pete Sessions (R), US Representative-Texas to the Committee on Oversight and Government Reform, March 14, 2016

Whereas magic is an art form with the unique power and potential to impact the lives of all people;

Whereas magic enables people to experience the impossible;

Whereas magic is used to inspire and bring wonder and happiness to others;

Whereas magic has had a significant impact on other art forms;

Whereas magic, like the great art forms of dance, literature, theater, film, and the visual arts, allows people to experience something that transcends the written word;

Whereas many technological advances can be directly traced to the influential work of magicians;

Whereas futurist Arthur C. Clarke claimed that any sufficiently advanced technology is indistinguishable from magic;

Whereas one of the greatest artists of all time, Leonardo da Vinci, was inspired by magic and co-wrote one of the very first books on magic in the late 15th century;

Whereas modern cinema would not exist today without the innovative work of the accomplished magician Georges Méliès;

Whereas magicians are visual storytellers who seamlessly interweave elements of mystery, wonder, emotion, and expression;

Whereas magic is an outstanding artistic model of individual expression;

Whereas magic fulfills some of the highest ideals and aspirations of our country by encouraging people to question what they believe and see;

Whereas magic is a unifying force across cultural, religious, ethnic, and age differences in our diverse Nation;

Whereas magic is an art that transforms the ordinary into the extraordinary;

Whereas the American magicians Harry Houdini and David Copperfield have been the most successful magicians of the past two centuries;

Whereas David Copperfield, introduced to magic as a boy growing up in New Jersey, has been named a Living Legend by the Library of Congress;

Whereas David Copperfield, with 21 Emmy Awards, 11 Guinness World Records, and over four billion dollars in ticket sales, has impacted every aspect of the global entertainment industry;

Whereas David Copperfield, through his magic, inspires great positive change in the lives of Americans;

Whereas people consistently leave David Copperfield's live magic show with a different perspective than when they entered;

Whereas Rebecca Brown of Portland, Oregon, left a David Copperfield magic show with a newfound inspiration to pursue her lifelong, unfulfilled passion for dance;

Whereas three months after Rebecca Brown attended the David Copperfield magic show, she performed her first choreographed recital in Portland, Oregon's Pioneer Square;

Whereas programs such as Project Magic, created by David Copperfield, use magic as a form of therapy for children with physical, psychological, and social disabilities;

Whereas learning magic through programs such as Project Magic can help these children improve their physical and mental dexterity and increase their confidence;

Whereas learning magic through programs such as Project Magic helps these children realize that they are no longer less able than their peers;

Whereas programs such as Project Magic teach these children that they are more capable and have a newfound ability to do what others cannot;

Whereas cities such as Wylie, Texas, and its mayor, Eric Hogue, recognize and promote the art of magic with official proclamations, summer educational programs, and the first festival dedicated to the art of magic in the State of Texas;

Whereas Mayor Eric Hogue, who learned the art of magic as a child, continues to use those skills to teach elementary school students about the different roles and responsibilities of local government;

Whereas magic is timeless in appeal and requires only the capacity to dream;

Whereas magic transcends any barrier of race, religion, language, or culture;

Whereas magic has not been properly recognized as a great American art form, nor has it been accorded the institutional status on a national level commensurate with its value and importance;

Whereas there is not an effective national effort to support and preserve magic;

Whereas documentation and archival support required by such a great art form has yet to be systematically applied to the field of magic; and

Whereas it is in the best interest of the national welfare to preserve and celebrate the unique art form of magic: Now, therefore, be it

Resolved, That the House of Representatives—

(1) recognizes magic as a rare and valuable art form and national treasure; and

(2) supports efforts to make certain that magic is preserved, understood, and promulgated.

Appendix 2: A Magic Proclamation

Full Text of Proclamation by Bill De Blasio, Mayor, City of New York, October 2017

OFFICE OF THE MAYOR
CITY OF NEW YORK

PROCLAMATION

Whereas:

As a global hub of creativity, New York offers a cultural landscape that is as diverse as our more than 8.5 million residents. Each night, performing artists of all disciplines thrill audiences across the five boroughs with their many talents — but only one entertainer shows up with a magical teapot. Tonight, one of New York's longest-running off-Broadway attractions, Chamber Magic, will celebrate its 5,000th show, and as you gather for an evening of conjuring, I am pleased to recognize its gifted creator and host, Steve Cohen, for his enchanting contributions to our city's dynamic performing arts sector.

Whereas:

It's no wonder that the most magical city in the world attracts and inspires the best magicians from near and far. As a boy growing up in Westchester, Steve Cohen became captivated by magic when his great uncle taught him his first trick at age six. He has diligently studied and practiced the craft ever since, becoming so skilled that he made it his profession. Cohen soon earned a following for his charming showmanship and his old-fashioned brand of magic, and in 2000 he began hosting solo shows for small audiences at the National Arts Club on Gramercy Park, before moving his increasingly in-demand Chamber Magic events to an ornate suite at the Waldorf-Astoria hotel. Modeled after the elegant parlor receptions in style at the turn of the 19th century, and limited to just 60 adults or youth ages 12 and up, these intimate gatherings allowed for a more interactive experience and up-close viewing of Cohen's masterful sleight-of-hand and his signature Think-a-Drink trick.

Whereas:

For the past 17 years, Chamber Magic has been dazzling sold-out audiences of New Yorkers and visitors who enjoy dressing up in fine attire for an evening of mystery and illusion presented by a magician wearing a top hat and tailcoat. When the show's longtime home, the Waldorf-Astoria, closed last year for renovations, Cohen ensured his critically-acclaimed act would go on at the Lotte New York Palace, another midtown landmark with a befitting classic atmosphere. On the occasion of the milestone 5,000th live performance of Chamber Magic, I am pleased to join with fans far and wide in applauding its ingenious star, Steve Cohen, for his efforts to enrich our city's cultural scene and engage and uplift people of all backgrounds through the mesmerizing art of magic.

Now therefore, I, Bill de Blasio, Mayor of the City of New York, do hereby proclaim Friday, October 6th, 2017 in the City of New York as:

"CHAMBER MAGIC DAY"

Signed,
Bill de Blasio
Mayor

Thank you for your purchase of this book!

As a token of my appreciation, I am pleased to provide you a FREE DOWNLOAD titled:

10 BEST LIVE MAGIC SHOWS
to see in the USA 2019-2010

Please visit the URL below to download your free copy.
https://magicalthebook.com/magicshows

And a quick final request: If you enjoyed this book, please leave your honest review on Amazon and do consider purchasing the ebook and audiobook versions.

As an author, I would like to hear from you, and your review provides me valuable information, feedback and encouragement. Your reviews and recommendations also help others like you to discover this book and related titles. Thank you in advance for your support. Read on!

Miscellaneous Links:

Book Website: https://magicalthebook.com/

Book Blog: https://magicalthebook.com/book-blog/

Amazon Author Page: http://amazon.com/author/bharatrao

Made in the USA
Middletown, DE
15 November 2019